"If you've ever felt like life pulls you in a thousand directions, *The Love Your Life Project* will be a breath of fresh air! Karen Ehman and Ruth Schwenk love Jesus and are here to guide you in rediscovering what really matters. More than just another self-help book—its wisdom and practical tips will teach us each to embrace the one life we've been given."

Candace Cameron Bure, actress, author,
and CEO of CandyRock Entertainment

"*The Love Your Life Project* challenges us to ask whether our lives line up with our words: Are we truly putting time into the things that matter most, or are we living distracted by lesser pursuits? Karen and Ruth gently coach readers to say yes to what is best and live in step with their values."

Phylicia Masonheimer, founder of Every Woman a Theologian

"*The Love Your Life Project* is a way back to the life we long for. Together, Karen and Ruth encourage us to allow Christ to shape our priorities, our callings, our daily routines, and even our rest. This book takes the truth of God's Word and makes it wonderfully practical, making this a resource you will want to pick up every single day."

Tara Sun, author of *Surrender Your Story*, and host
of the *Truth Talks with Tara* podcast

"In this power-packed book, Ruth and Karen share secrets to cultivating a life lived on purpose, while still creating space for rest. Want fresh inspiration and doable action steps to not just survive life but to actually thrive? This book is a must-read!"

Crystal Paine, mom of six, *New York Times* bestselling author,
and founder of Money Saving Mom

"What a rich resource of scriptural wisdom and practical tools Karen and Ruth have provided for us! I have watched these ladies live out the truths of *The Love Your Life Project* in their personal lives, so I know this book will be a powerful tool in the hands of any woman who wants to develop habits aligning with her priorities while also embracing the rest God provides."

Courtney Joseph Fallick, author of *Still Standing* and blogger
at WomenLivingWell.org, the home of Good Morning Girls

"In a culture where we have every opportunity to fill our hearts and minds with activities, aspirations, and temporary happiness apart from Christ, *The Love Your Life Project* cuts to the root of where and how to center our joy. This book does an amazing job of grounding its readers in the joys of Christ by calling into question the sometimes subtle, sometimes overt ways we fill our lives with distractions and busyness."

Chelsea Damon, author of *I Thought This Would Make Me Happy*
and *Together with Christ: A Dating Couple's Devotional*

the love your life project

Books by Karen Ehman and Ruth Schwenk
from Bethany House Publishers

Trusting God in All the Things by Karen Ehman and Ruth Schwenk

Reach Out, Gather In by Karen Ehman

Make Their Day by Karen Ehman

Jesus, Calm My Heart by Ruth Schwenk

The Bedtime Family Devotional by Ruth and Patrick Schwenk

The Love Your Life Project by Karen Ehman and Ruth Schwenk

the love your life project

40 DAYS TO PRIORITIZE
YOUR PASSIONS, CULTIVATE PRODUCTIVE HABITS, AND REFUEL WITH TIMES OF REST

KAREN EHMAN
AND RUTH SCHWENK

BETHANYHOUSE
a division of Baker Publishing Group
Minneapolis, Minnesota

© 2024 by Karen Ehman and Ruth Schwenk

Published by Bethany House Publishers
Minneapolis, Minnesota
BethanyHouse.com

Bethany House Publishers is a division of
Baker Publishing Group, Grand Rapids, Michigan

Printed in the United States of America

Library of Congress Cataloging-in-Publication Data
Names: Ehman, Karen, author. | Schwenk, Ruth, author.
Title: The love your life project : 40 days to prioritize your passions, cultivate productive
    habits, and refuel with times of rest / by Karen Ehman and Ruth Schwenk.
Description: Minneapolis, Minnesota : Bethany House Publishers, a division of Baker
    Publishing Group, [2024] | Includes bibliographical references.
Identifiers: LCCN 2023054048 | ISBN 9780764242977 (paper) | ISBN 9780764244162
    (cloth) | ISBN 9781493446759 (ebook)
Subjects: LCSH: Life—Religious aspects—Christianity. | Self-acceptance—Religious
    aspects—Christianity. | Meaning (Philosophy) —Religious aspects—Christianity. | Rest—
    Religious aspects—Christianity.
Classification: LCC BV4501.3 .E39592 2024 | DDC 248.4—dc23/eng/20240205
LC record available at https://lccn.loc.gov/2023054048

Cover Design: Micaela Blankenship
Ruth Schwenk author photo © Kelsie Johanna Photography

The authors are represented by the Brock, Inc. Agency.

Baker Publishing Group publications use paper produced from sustainable forestry practices and postconsumer waste whenever possible.

24 25 26 27 28 29 30   7 6 5 4 3 2 1

In Loving Memory of
Patrick William Schwenk
Beloved Husband, Father, Pastor, and Friend
February 27, 1975 – January 5, 2024

He served God. He loved others.
In both life and death,
he showed us how to live our priorities.

contents

Karen   Ruth

Section Three: Pursuing the Passions God Has for Me 117

Section Four: Finding My Follow-Through 163

INTRODUCTION

We never grow closer to God when we just live life. It takes deliberate pursuit and attentiveness.

Francis Chan, *Crazy Love*

Imagine you've been assigned to bake a birthday cake for your best friend's upcoming party. You decide a German chocolate cake sounds like a winner, with its deep, moist, chocolatey inside and its decadent, caramelized coconut-pecan frosting. In fact, you know your friend will be pleased because it is her absolutely favorite dessert. So you don your apron and head to the kitchen to whip up this culinary masterpiece.

How strange it would be if you just began pulling random staples from the cupboard that you *think* might go into the cake. You know it takes flour, sugar, and cocoa powder, and you're pretty sure there's vanilla and baking soda. Or is it baking powder? You also can't quite remember if it takes oil or butter, and the only thing you know for certain about the frosting is that coconut and pecans are involved. Nevertheless, you have your assignment, so you cross your fingers and toss the ingredients into a bowl expectantly—and with quite a bit of trepidation. After all, you're not only unsure of what all goes into the cake, you have no idea of the exact measurements or of in what order to add them. You are clueless as to the temperature and time for baking. Now, how do you think that cake will turn out? Most likely, it will be a total flop.

Sadly, for a lot of us, our life is like that cake.

We know that life consists of people and projects, of work and play, and lots of duties to be done around the house. And of course, we surmise the most important part of life is our journey of faith that we began when we first responded to the gospel and placed our trust in Christ. But for many of us, we have no plan, no playbook—no real recipe for life. Instead of living out our days with forethought, attention, and intention, we simply take life as it comes, reacting to what is thrown our way and hoping for the best. Of course, we seek to spiritualize it by glazing it with a thin Jesus-y coat of religion. We read our devotions. We go to church. We say our prayers at night—that is if we don't fall asleep first from exhaustion. But we never seem to get better at living or grow closer to God as the years march on. And we certainly never learn to refuel with times of real and deep rest—both physical and emotional. As a result, we find ourselves struggling to experience joy.

New York Times bestselling author Dr. Henry Cloud is an expert in the secret of happiness that can be found only in God. After doing extensive research about happiness and fulfillment in life, he commented, "I read study after study, which were proving that happiness and fulfillment is not found in our circumstances, our bank accounts, our material possessions, or achievements. Instead, what the research revealed was that happiness comes largely from how we live our lives and into which activities we decide to invest our hearts, minds, souls, and strength."[1]

Our prayer for you is that the resource you hold in your hands will serve as a recipe book of sorts, pointing you to Jesus, the founder and finisher of our faith who can empower us to run the race set before us (Hebrews 12:1–2). As you lay the various components of your life before him prayerfully, he will enable you to live your days with intention and strengthen your relationships with love, honesty, and grace. The result will be a life lived for God that allows you to experience deep joy.

The Love Your Life Project is more than just a book to read. It is also a tool to incorporate into your daily life that will help you learn to live your priorities and love your life. It is designed to be part workbook—you will work through some biblical content, evaluate your practices of the past, and make productive plans for the future—and part journal. The journaling aspect will enable you to unearth and organize your thoughts, hopes, fears, and dreams. You'll also notice that each day includes a Dig Deeper suggestion. These book, podcast, or other resource recommendations will help you to build a list of other useful tools that you may utilize to further explore the topic of that particular day, should you desire. There is also a section at the back of the book where you can record notes for loving your life.

By the end of the forty days, you will have discovered your passions and thoroughly evaluated your current habits and practices for getting life done. But most important, you will also have come up with a doable plan for cultivating productive habits and refueling with times of rest. Also, if you prefer not to hike solo on this journey but to trek alongside others, be sure to check out the Leader's Guide at the back of the book. It will equip you to gather and guide a group of women who will support and encourage each other as you all learn to live your priorities and love your life.

So grab a Bible and a pen. Pour yourself a steaming cup of creamy, hot deliciousness, or some refreshing iced tea on the rocks. Prepare to learn how to be prepared. Expect to grow your faith in God and deepen your walk with Jesus. Anticipate all the Holy Spirit will do in your heart to encourage and strengthen you, pointing you to where you might touch the lives of others as you live out your ordinary days here on earth.

May your life be a vivid testimony of God's goodness. May his constant guidance bring you comfort and infuse your life with authentic joy rather than temporary situational happiness. You can learn to love your life; the life your Creator has already planned for you, full of faith and good works (Ephesians 2:10).

Thank you for the honor of walking beside you on this remarkable excursion.

In His Great Love,

Karen and Ruth

Determining My Priorities

The first step in learning to live your priorities and love your life is discovering what your priorities actually are. In the first ten days of our time together, we will take a detailed look at your life, including how you spend your time, with whom your paths naturally intersect, and your current plan (or lack thereof) for living.

Work your way slowly through each day, carefully examining Scriptures and earnestly answering the reflection questions posed. An important part of each day is taking the time to write out a heartfelt prayer to God about the subject of the day. Don't skip over that part! Expect God to answer your prayers as you seek to live your life in a way that honors him and points others to Jesus.

The Alphabet of Life

KAREN

I recently hit "follow" on a social media account that provides me a bit of nostalgic fun. The posts all revisit the period when I was in middle and high school. They may show a television commercial that was popular, a fashion trend that was hot, a well-loved food item, or other such tidbit of reminiscence. Seeing the images makes me smile. (And, if I'm being honest, sometimes make me feel a little old!)

The other day, the account featured the cover of a popular magazine for teen girls that I read faithfully in high school. In fact, the minute I saw the post, I not only recognized the cover, but I remembered the spread of back-to-school clothing from JCPenney that was showcased in its interior pages. Oh, how I'd longed to dress like the smiling models in the magazine. I remember circling the outfits I wished I could go to the mall and buy.

However, it wasn't just the clothing I'd yearned for back then. Helpful articles told of tips and tricks for success as a teenager: how to get more out of your study time, the proper way to apply your makeup, how to get along with your parents, and—of course—how to attract the attention of that certain guy you hoped would ask you to the homecoming dance.

Even at that young age, I was trying to find success in the various components of my everyday life. I clipped articles, circled pictures, wrote in my diary, and began keeping a planner to not only track my social events, but keep me on schedule for studying. I thought if I just applied all that I discovered, I could live all parts of life well.

I am not so far from my teenage self. Pick any year of my adult life— whether it was in college, when I was first married, my days as a new mom, or today, now that my children are all older—I still shoot for success in the various areas of life, thinking somehow it comes from the outside in; that if I can just unearth the best time-management tips, or house-hold hacks, or health and beauty secrets—not to mention faith-based shortcuts that will catapult my spiritual growth—then my life will be happy and whole.

However, after three decades of adulting, I have learned an important truth: getting your life together does not come from the outside in, simply applying principles you learn. Instead, it comes from the inside out: learning to prayerfully set—and then carefully live out—your priorities, accepting the life that results.

So, how do we decide what our priorities are? Psalm 111:10 is a fantastic starting place. Here it is in the Amplified version of the Bible. (This version helps to highlight the intended meaning of the original Hebrew or Greek words that were used in the initial manuscripts.)

> The [reverent] fear of the Lord is the beginning (the
>   prerequisite, the absolute essential, the alphabet) of wisdom;
> A good understanding and a teachable heart are possessed by
>   all those who do the will of the Lord;
> His praise endures forever.

If we want to properly live out our priorities, we first need to obtain wisdom. And the first step in obtaining wisdom is the reverent fear of the Lord. I love the picture that is painted in the original Hebrew word for *beginning.* That word is *reshith* (pronounced *ray-sheeth'*) and it means the foremost, the finest, or the choicest. It is the prerequisite of life, with everything else hinging upon it. Not only is it essential, but it is considered the alphabet. What does this mean?

Our success begins with our understanding the fear of the Lord, living it out daily, and returning to it when we stray.

Think about the alphabet for a moment. When a young child is being taught to read, the first step is to learn, understand, and memorize the letters of the alphabet, including the sounds they make and how they affect other letters and their sounds. A child's future reading success hinges upon acquiring this knowledge. It is much the same with living our life God's way. Our success begins with our understanding the fear of the Lord, living it out daily, and returning to it when we stray.

In our Day 2 entry, we will look specifically at whether what we say our priorities are syncs up with how we spend our time. But for today, let's explore the foundation, the alphabet of life—the reverent fear of the Lord that leads to wisdom.

- When it comes to finding success in the various areas of your life, what approach have you been taking? List below any places, people, or resources to which you usually turn. That may be studying the Bible. It may be trusted mentors. But it also might be social media, articles on the Internet, a popular pastor or teacher, or a particular book.

- How well have these worked for you in helping you to live life fully and in a way that honors God and satisfies you?

- *The fear of the Lord* is sometimes a misunderstood term. There are two words translated from Hebrew to English as *fear* in the Old Testament—*charadah* and *yirah* (pronounced *khar-aw-daw'* and *yir-aw'*). *Charadah* means to tremble with colossal apprehension or to feel excessive dread. *Yirah*, on the other hand, means to react with immense awe, considerate respect, and reverence. This second word—*yirah*—is used when describing the fear of the Lord. This response means respecting God enough to observe his commands. It is treating him—and his holy Word—with the utmost reverence. How might you write in your own words what it means to fear the Lord? Use the space below to do so.

- When you think of wisdom in your life, what comes to mind? Is it something you think you naturally possess simply because you follow Christ? Do you make seeking wisdom a matter of prayer, asking God for it often? Do you feel that you understand what wisdom is? (Hint: It is not the same thing as knowledge, which centers on gathering facts and knowing information, data, or theories.)

- Look up the following verses in Scripture that speak of wisdom. After each one, jot down any thoughts you may have in the space provided.

  James 1:5

  Proverbs 16:16

  Proverbs 11:2

  2 Timothy 2:7

- Finally, take a few minutes to craft a prayer to God, asking him for wisdom. Weave in the various thoughts you recorded about the verses you looked up. Ask him to make this forty-day journey not only a time of discovery, but also a pivotal time in your life when you purposefully place him at the center as you prioritize your passions, cultivate productive habits, and refuel with times of rest.

• My Prayer •

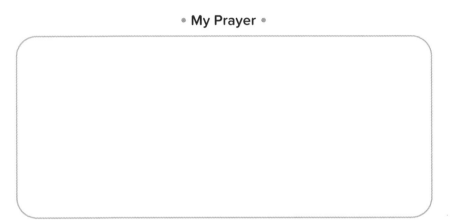

• Dig Deeper •

Listen to the *Daily Grace* podcast, episode 135: "What Does It Mean to Fear the Lord?"

• Highlighted Verse •

The [reverent] fear of the Lord is the beginning (the
    prerequisite, the absolute essential, the alphabet) of wisdom;
A good understanding and a teachable heart are possessed by
    all those who do the will of the Lord;
His praise endures forever.

                                            Psalm 111:10 AMP

day 2

Priority Treatment

KAREN

One day several years ago, a mentor of mine asked me a sobering question one day: "Does how you spend your time actually line up with what you say your priorities are?" I had to admit that many days, it didn't. While I might assert that my relationship with God was my highest priority, followed by those in my family, and then others, often I was letting the more trivial activities of life—consuming media, hobbies, or even wasting time putting items I'd probably never end up buying in an online shopping cart—crowd out that which I claimed was more important.

We hear a lot of talk about priorities—at work, at home, in our relationships, and in our responsibilities. We long to keep our priorities straight, but it isn't always easy to do with our busy schedules and in our often frenzied culture.

If someone were to ask you to list your priorities, you might put God first, your close family members second, followed by work, friends, and so on down the list. However, often the reality of our behavior—how we spend our time and where we focus our energies—depicts quite a different scenario.

Psalm 90:12 addresses how we spend our time and live out our days: "Teach us to number our days carefully so that we may develop wisdom in our hearts" (csb). In the original Hebrew, the word translated "number" here is *manah* (pronounced *maw-naw'*) and it means to assign, to appoint, to prepare, or to reckon. The root word that it originally comes from offers even deeper insight, indicating properly weighing out or allotting our days in an intentional way.

These more precise shades of meaning show that we are not to just take our days as they come, plodding through life in a haphazard way. We are to give careful thought to how we spend our time daily—preparing for these days, assigning meaning and purpose to them in an intentional way.

What is the result of doing this? We "develop wisdom in our hearts." The Hebrew word for wisdom—*chokmah* (pronounced *khok-maw'*)—means not just to be wise, but also encompasses the concept of possessing shrewd insight in life or superior skill in war. Who among us couldn't use shrewd insight into living our lives—which on some days do have us feeling as though we are embroiled in a battle?

> **Does how you spend your time actually line up with what you say your priorities are?**

Today we will work through an exercise designed to help you clearly determine your priorities. It will also equip you to remove any tasks, activities, or responsibilities that are on your plate but shouldn't be, so they can stop crowding out time for what is truly important.

First, fill in the list below with the people, tasks, and responsibilities you have, ranking them in order of greatest priority. Don't forget to include your relationship with God. (We have given the number seven as a suggestion, but you may have more or fewer than that.)

My Priorities

1.

2.

3.

4.

5.

6.

7.

Now, take an honest look at your list. Do what you claim to be your top priorities line up with how you spend your time? Of course, you can't determine this merely by the number of minutes or hours you spend on each one. If you must put in forty hours a week at a job, you don't have any wiggle room on that. Pay closer attention to the amount of focus, energy, and prayer you place on each one and how attentive you are to the needs and feelings of the people on the list. Does your list line up with how you spend your time? To determine this, work through these next steps.

- Glance back over the list. Underline any priorities that you believe are getting the proper measure of your focus, time, and energy.
- Next, circle any of the priorities that you feel are not receiving adequate attention.

- Finally, place a star next to the priority you most want to focus on improving in the coming weeks.
- Why did you choose the one you starred? What, specifically, would you like to see change when it comes to that priority in your life?

Next, let's examine the commitments you have said yes to that are outside your four walls. Are you involved in activities at church? In the community? At your children's schools? Is there a hobby or outside interest that takes up your time each month? List all your various commitments in the space below. Then do the exercise following it.

My Commitments

- Examine your listed commitments. Prayerfully ask the Lord if there is anything on the list that you should bow out of. (The world will still go on.) If you sense something needs to go, place an X through it. Circle any commitments you confidently feel God calling you to keep. Place a question mark beside any you are unsure of.
- Commit to praying about those responsibilities for the next week, asking God if they should stay or go. Also ask God to reveal to you whether you should carry out a commitment for the remainder of the year or term, but not sign up to do it again.
- Finally, take the next few moments to craft out a prayer to God about living your priorities, making sure how you spend your time lines up with what you say the priorities are. He is faithful to listen and help you in this endeavor.

• My Prayer •

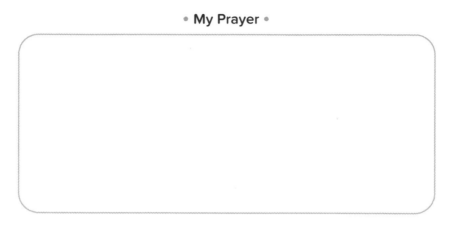

• Dig Deeper •

Listen to the *Rhythms for Life* podcast with Rebekah and Gabe Lyons, "Knowing God's Plan for Your Life: Pete Richardson."

• Highlighted Verse •

Teach us to number our days carefully
so that we may develop wisdom in our hearts.

Psalm 90:12 CSB

day 3

Your Most Important Priority

RUTH

My head is usually already spinning the minute I wake up. My thoughts are racing. Before my feet even hit the floor, my mind is already being pulled in a thousand different directions! With so many priorities come so many possibilities.

Where do I even begin?
What is most important to do first?
Which is the "priority among priorities"?

But before we get too far, I want to simply point out that the kind of priority I am talking about here is not so much about something we need to *do*, but rather about a perspective we need to *have*. Priority is first and foremost about perspective—not something I do, but something I have. The perspective that Jesus reminds us to have first is this: that his kingdom—or his calling on our life—comes first. In Matthew 6:33–34 we read,

But seek first his kingdom and his righteousness, and all these things will be given to you as well. Therefore do not worry about tomorrow, for tomorrow will worry about itself. Each day has enough trouble of its own.

As human beings, we are called by God. God has invited us to live *with* him and *for* him. And his calling—as mysterious as that can feel to us—comes to us each day. Many times it shows up in the ordinary and mundane events of today. So our first priority is to have the perspective that what is most important today is whatever Jesus is asking me to be faithful with.

It could be something as simple as laundry. A meeting at work. Lunch with a friend. Time with kids. A conversation with a neighbor. The other day, I read a quote widely attributed to St. Therese of Lisieux and thought it was so good—and of course, so challenging: "Nothing except for today."[1] That is our first priority! God's call for each of us to listen to him comes today. Tomorrow will worry about itself, Jesus said. To be sure, each day has enough trouble of its own.

I can get so caught up—worrying about tomorrow or the next month, work, family, and the list goes on! But the life of true freedom, joy, and peace is found in taking Jesus at his word. *Today.*

> **Priority is first and foremost about perspective—not something I do, but something I have.**

While we might feel tired and isolated at times, we are not alone. Our story, or day for that matter, is not spiraling out of control. There is a God who is present and purposeful in all things. There is a sacred history, or kingdom, behind and beyond our own—beyond our politics, greater than our nations, and even bigger than all our suffering and tasks and responsibilities. So we ask God for the grace to be faithful today, while trusting him for tomorrow. What matters most? What is our priority?

It is not, first and foremost, something we do; it is a way of thinking. It is a perspective or posture we must have if we are to love our life, a life oriented around Jesus. This is, after all, the abundant life Jesus promised (John 10:10).

Our motivation, the way of living that truly brings life, is bent toward doing what God wants right here and right now—today. And so, maybe even before we get out of bed, we simply pray, "Lord, I give you today. Be in charge. I trust you for tomorrow. Give me grace to be faithful to you today."

Let's explore how we move from seeing a priority as something we need to *do* to understanding a priority as a perspective we need to *have.*

Changing How We Think

- What are the top two or three priorities from the lists you created on Day 2 that can quickly crowd and consume your thoughts, attention, and energy each day?

- Practically speaking, how can you change the way you view priorities?

- While we can't pull out of all our daily tasks and responsibilities, how can having a perspective of "nothing except for today" change what you do each day?

- How can focusing on faithfulness today bring freedom?

Take some time to read Matthew 6:25–34. Focus on verses 33–34 and Jesus' call to give him today and to seek God's kingdom first. Once you have done this, reflect on the following questions:

- What does Jesus promise if we seek first his kingdom?
- How is this perspective countercultural? In other words, what makes our living this way so different from those around us?
- Identify several priorities that are causing you to lose perspective and peace.
- Spend a few minutes prayerfully considering how you can practically guard against living in tomorrow.

Take the next few moments to write out a prayer. Maybe this is a time to confess how other priorities have become more important than living for Jesus. Perhaps this is an opportunity to ask for God's grace to trust him. Or maybe this is a prayer of surrender and a renewed desire to see what God sees as important each day.

• My Prayer •

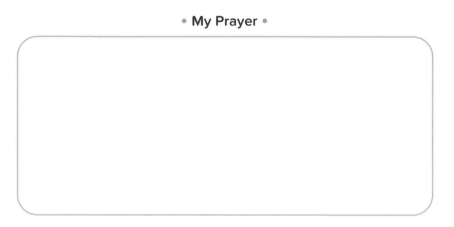

• Dig Deeper •

Check out the helpful app One Minute Pause by John Eldredge, which offers one-minute, three-minute, and five-minute pauses (along with others of varying lengths) designed to help you release everything to God and reconnect with him.

• Highlighted Verses •

But seek first his kingdom and his righteousness, and all these things will be given to you as well. Therefore do not worry about tomorrow, for tomorrow will worry about itself. Each day has enough trouble of its own.

Matthew 6:33–34

Those who are **wise** have thought about the path they are on.

They have given **consideration** to the day ahead, or weeks and months beyond.

A life well lived, one we love, is rooted in living out this **wisdom** in a variety of ways.

We are living on purpose: internally and proactively, **God's way.**

day 4

The Power of Predetermination

RUTH

We pulled up into the store parking lot. Since our kids were very young at the time, I knew I was in for a challenge. There was the toy aisle. The dollar section. And of course, the dreaded candy display at the checkout. Any of those sections could spell disaster!

I quickly began to think through a plan. *Here is where I need to go*, I thought. *This is what I need to get.* Then I began to explain the plan to our kids. "Mom needs to grab a few items. We are not getting any toys or candy today. Everyone needs to be good listeners and be sure to stay with me. No running or screaming when we are in the store. Be sure to smile and say hello to the checkout person when they greet you." You get the point. You can probably visualize the deer-in-the-headlights looks I received from my children.

But oddly enough, it worked! Not perfectly. But in time, this type of planning ahead or predetermination saved us a lot of headaches. There really is something to the simple discipline of thinking and planning ahead. It's the power of predetermination.

It's easy to fall into the trap of living externally instead of internally. When we live externally, we are always responding to what is outside of us. Or around us. We might say that we live reactive lives instead of proactive lives. When we are living externally, we are allowing others to determine and direct our priorities and plans for us.

It might look like any of these:

A steady stream of emails.
Text messages.
Maybe a co-worker who pops in unexpectedly.
A phone call.
Family needs.
A friend who just has to stop by . . . *right now*.

All of these have the potential to steer us off course. While each of these can be legitimate and necessary, the challenge is always to come back to what is driving us internally. To live internally is to live with clarity and commitment to the priorities you have set in your life. Whatever the external need is, predetermination will help us stay focused, or get refocused when we have to.

> **To live internally is to live with clarity and commitment to the priorities you have set in your life.**

Throughout the Bible, we are often confronted with a choice. We are given the reminder that there are two ways to live—we can walk in wisdom or foolishness. This theme that weaves its way through Scripture begins in the Garden of Eden. Adam and Eve are given a choice. Will they do life God's way or their way?

This theme of wisdom versus foolishness is especially clear in the Old Testament book of Proverbs. These pieces of wisdom seek to give us instruction on how life generally works. These short truths are not always a guarantee, but they are meant to teach us how life usually works if we walk according to God's plans and purposes.

And one of these proverbs has to do with planning ahead. Skillful living, or wise living, involves thinking ahead—what we are calling predetermination. Proverbs 13:16 points out that "All who are prudent act with knowledge, but fools expose their folly."

The proverb is telling us that those who are wise have thought about the path they are on. They have given consideration to the day ahead, or weeks and months beyond. A life well lived, one we love, is rooted in living out this wisdom in a variety of ways. As it relates to our priorities and calling, it means we are thinking and acting with knowledge. We don't just wing it! We are living on purpose: internally and proactively, God's way.

So what does it look like to live with predetermination?

It might resemble some of the following:

- Reviewing your schedule and priorities each morning.
- Predetermining the tasks that take priority by listing them out in order.
- Communicating expectations about your schedule or plans in advance to those around you.

Every day we have a choice: Will we live *externally* or *internally*? Will we live out *our* priorities or someone else's? Put into practice the habit of predetermination!

Today, let's spend some time looking at ways we live externally instead of internally. How can we move from living reactively to living proactively?

Below is a series of questions to help you see more clearly how there is power in predetermination.

Living Externally vs. Internally

- In your own words, what does it mean to live externally?

- What are the most common things that cause you to live externally?

- What are two or three simple habits each day that could help you live internally?

- What area of your life most needs the simple discipline of predetermination?

Two key Scriptures for today are Proverbs 13:16 and Luke 14:28–30. Take some time to read these verses and consider them in their context. Once you have done this, reflect on the following questions:

- What do these passages have in common?
- What is the value in both of these passages of considering the cost or acting with knowledge?
- In its original context, Luke 14:28–30 is about considering the cost of being a disciple. How do these verses most apply to living out your priorities or God's calling in your life right now?
- Describe a time when you did not practice predetermination and the impact that had on others. How can predetermination best benefit those around you?

Take the next few moments to write out a prayer. Ask God to help you act with prudence. Share how you long to live with greater clarity, more internally and less externally.

• My Prayer •

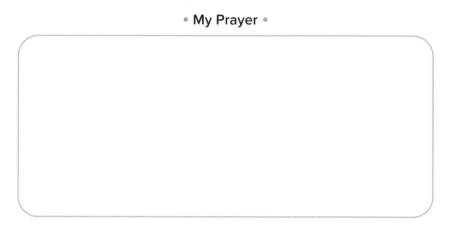

• Dig Deeper •

Read *The Art of Living Well: A Biblical Approach from Proverbs* by Kenneth Boa and Gail Burnett.

• Highlighted Verse •

All who are prudent act with knowledge, but fools expose their folly.

Proverbs 13:16

day 5

Saying No to Say Yes!

RUTH

My husband and I have been in local church ministry for nearly twenty-five years. We've led youth groups and mission trips, planted a church, opened our home countless times, held newborn babies at the hospital, prayed with people before surgeries, done crisis counseling, and more. In so many different ways, we have had the privilege to be involved in people's lives.

And as you know—from your own experience and circumstances—there is no shortage of need! This is both the joy and the challenge of doing what Jesus calls us to do. The mark of a disciple or follower of Jesus is to love God and love others. So saying no feels funny. It can feel wrong. As a result, we can say yes a lot.

Saying yes can be easy for me. After all, I love people! But is answering in the affirmative ever a bad thing? Maybe you have caught yourself sounding a bit like this:

"Yes, my husband and I can lead a small group, especially since it is a really big need right now."

"No big deal if you can't find anyone else, I can be the secretary for the school PTO."

"Sure, I can help plan the meals for church."

"Wow! I would really love to be in that Bible study. Let me think about it, but I probably can."

"Sure, I can help plan the annual work Christmas party."

Those are a lot of yeses! Sound familiar? Yes, yes, yes, sure, yes, okay, yes! So, again, is answering yes ever a bad thing? Well, let me ask you . . . Are you overcommitted? Does your schedule feel pretty packed—almost to the point that there is not much room left?

36

There is an interesting story and illustration about saying no. Oddly enough, it comes from Jesus. In Mark 1 we read about how he had gotten up early to pray and be alone. When his disciples go and find him, they explain that everyone is looking for him! In other words, there is more work to do! More need. And more opportunities to say yes.

Mark 1:36–38 says,

> Simon and his companions went to look for him, and when they found him, they exclaimed: "Everyone is looking for you!"
>
> Jesus replied, "Let us go somewhere else—to the nearby villages—so I can preach there also. That is why I have come."

Did you catch what just happened? In verse 38 Jesus says, "Let us go somewhere else." He moves away from the massive needs that were mounting. He moves toward his purpose. By saying no, he was actually saying yes to his purpose, which Jesus identifies as his preaching: "That is why I have come."

Jesus' no to the pressure of some people was actually a yes to his purpose for others. His no wasn't to get away or skirt responsibilities. His no wasn't getting him away from people. The Lord's no enabled him to be able to give himself more fully and faithfully to others.

> **Jesus' no to the pressure of some people was actually a yes to his purpose for others.**

My personality draws me to be a part of every opportunity and every need that comes my way. But I want to encourage you today and tell you it is okay to say no.

No for your own soul.

No for your own schedule.

Maybe even a no for your own marriage or family or job.

But ultimately, saying no helps you say yes to love others more fully and faithfully and in a way that is more consistent with your purpose and season of life.

There are times when we must say yes to Jesus and yes to sacrificially serving others. And yet there are also times, even seasons, when we need to discern when to say no. There is freedom in not saying yes to every single thing that comes our way. We come to realize that in saying no, we are actually saying a greater and better yes.

Today, let's try to discern more clearly what season we might be in. Let's ask the Holy Spirit to give us wisdom to know when to say no and when to say yes.

Examining Our Opportunities

- Which best describes you right now and why: "I have a lot to give" or "I have very little to give."

- What life circumstances contribute to your current season?

- Identify two or three commitments that may not be necessary right now.

- Prayerfully consider the difference between calling and opportunity. Not all opportunities are necessarily God's calling. Is there an opportunity you have said yes to that may not be what God is calling you to do right now?

A key passage for today is Mark 1:35–39. Take some time to read this passage slowly. Pay attention to what Jesus does. Notice what he doesn't do.

- In this passage, what is Jesus saying no to?

- How is Jesus' answer of no connected to his purpose?

- What is the difference between saying no for our sake and saying no for the sake of others?

- What do you notice about Jesus' perspective and practice of being alone that can help you live with greater love for others?

Take the next few moments to write out a prayer. Ask God to give you wisdom to discern those difficult decisions of saying no or yes.

• My Prayer •

• Dig Deeper •

Read *Boundaries for Your Soul: How to Turn Your Overwhelming Thoughts and Feelings into Your Greatest Allies* by Dr. Alison Cook and Kimberly Miller.

• Highlighted Verse •

Jesus replied, "Let us go somewhere else—to the nearby villages—so I can preach there also. That is why I have come."

Mark 1:38

day 6

Is God Saying No, Go, or Slow?

KAREN

"That sounds like fun. Of course I'll be there. I wouldn't miss it for the world!" This answer tumbled off my lips when someone asked me to attend a huge moms conference being held in the Midwest when my children were all tiny. They mentioned it was going to be coming up at the beginning of the new year, sometime in January. I didn't have any travel plans for work or any other commitments on any weekend that month that I knew of, so I assumed I would be able to attend.

However, when a few weeks passed and the registration forms were posted, my heart sank. This fabulous event I was so looking forward to attending would fall smack dab on something I'd completely overlooked— my oldest son's fifth birthday! Now I was faced with a dilemma. A few of my friends suggested we celebrate his big day a week early. However, I knew this little guy was sharp and would know that the party was not taking place on his actual birthday. So I declined attending, even though I wanted to go so badly. Instead, I stayed home and served pizza and homemade birthday cake to about a dozen or so smiling young boys. My son's smile was the biggest.

After I became a mom, it took me a while to find my groove as far as commitments outside my home were concerned. My personality tends to value busyness and achievement, and I often pack my days too tightly. Once I became a mom, I thought I would just strap my child in a baby carrier and take her along for the ride. However, some health conditions and general colickiness prevented this from happening. I was forced to slow down, reevaluate, and face the realization that I had limitations. I simply couldn't keep running at the pace I was used to.

As women, we are not limitless and inexhaustible. (I know—shocker!) We can't keep running at breakneck speed and think we won't suffer because of it. We only have so much time, energy, and margin in our lives.

So with each season—and even with every activity or commitment—we need to ask ourselves, "What is God saying: no, go, or slow?"

There certainly are times when we feel we are being given the green light to say yes to a responsibility, to help with an event or activity, or to commit to a task. However, there are other times when we need to fiercely guard the margins in our life, declining to put any further items onto our calendar. A third approach can be employed when we feel permission to take something on, but we do it carefully, methodically, and slowly, making sure not to bite off more than we can chew.

> **So with each season—and even with every activity or commitment—we need to ask ourselves, "What is God saying: no, go, or slow?"**

In Jeremiah 33:3, we are told that the word of the Lord came to Jeremiah. He said, in part, "Call to me and I will answer you and tell you great and incomprehensible things you do not know" (csb). The same God who spoke those words to the prophet is also available to listen to our pleas today. Maybe you "do not know" what answer you should give to the person asking you to take on a task or responsibility. What should you do? *Call on God.* Perhaps a seemingly amazing opportunity is being offered to you, and it makes the most business sense to say yes, but you feel the tug of your precious family time nudging you to say no. What should you do? *Call on him.* Our Father is faithful. He will answer us if we humbly and diligently seek him.

In the case of my son's fifth birthday party, I knew I needed to say a resounding no to attending the conference. However, years later, I was asked to be a speaker at a different conference the weekend of that same child's thirteenth birthday. But this time, two of his favorite Christian bands were appearing at the conference, and I was able to obtain backstage passes for him and his brother to meet them and get their pictures taken. In this instance, I felt permission to say yes, because saying yes would also please and encourage my son.

Here are some questions to contemplate when deciding whether you are in a season of no, go, or slow:

- First, have you prayed about it? I know this sounds simplistic, but it is the most important starting point. Remember, wisdom is the foundation for a life well lived. Ask God for wisdom in this particular decision.
- Have you made a list of pros and cons? Doing this the old-fashioned way on paper can help you see whether you should say yes or no to what you are being asked to do. It might also help you realize that you may be able to assist with a small

portion of what is being requested of you, though not the entire responsibility. This would be the "slow" answer.

- Have you factored in what saying yes might do to your other responsibilities and relationships at home, at work, and in your church and community? Sometimes we add more to our plate without removing something already there. We think we are just so creative and clever that if we rearrange everything, somehow, we can make it all fit. But every time you say yes to something new, it impacts the commitments you already have, so think those over carefully.

- Have you sought the advice of any trusted friends or wise mentors? Laying out all the facts for them may enable you to see an angle you'd not noticed before. Because these people are not emotionally or historically tied to the facts of the decision, they can offer a fresh perspective.

- Finally, read over the following verses that talk about God's willingness to answer us when we call upon him. Jot your thoughts after each verse that pertain to seeking an answer for your situation.

1 Chronicles 16:11

Psalm 9:10

Psalm 40:16

Luke 11:9–10

Psalm 32:8

- Think about a situation in your life currently in which you have
  been asked to take on something or you have a task you are considering implementing. Go over the questions above and try to
  determine if your answer will be no, go, or slow. Record the situation here and then write what your answer will be: no, go, or slow.

The situation:

My answer:

Time to pray! In the space provided, compose a prayer you can whis-
per each morning about the commitments and responsibilities you will
be asked to take on in life. In it, seek wisdom from God about discerning
when he is calling you to do something and you should say yes, or when
it is best that you pass up the obligation. Also ask for discernment for
those times when you will go slow—either taking on only a portion of a
responsibility or proceeding very slowly with the task at hand.

• My Prayer •

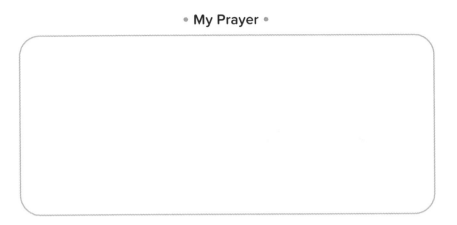

• Dig Deeper •

Read *Don't Overthink It: Make Easier Decisions, Stop Second-Guessing, and Bring More Joy to Your Life* by Anne Bogel.

• Highlighted Verses •

While he was still confined in the guard's courtyard, the word of the Lord came to Jeremiah a second time: "The Lord who made the earth, the Lord who forms it to establish it, the Lord is his name, says this: Call to me and I will answer you and tell you great and incomprehensible things you do not know."

Jeremiah 33:1–3 CSB

day 7

Turning a Discipline into a Desire

RUTH

They were a few tables down from us in a crowded restaurant that day—a couple who were at least forty years ahead of us in marriage. But what caught our attention wasn't that they sat alone, as we were sitting, but that they sat silent.

In those early years of our marriage, words came easily. We talked about family, ministry, food, and just about everything else you can imagine! So it surprised us—and I would say it even saddened us—to see a marriage without words. No chatter. Seemingly no communication, which is where we made our mistake in assumption.

I remember my husband (who freely admits now that he spoke with ignorance) leaned in toward the middle of our table and whispered, "We'll never be like that." What he meant was we'd always have something to say. Words would never be a struggle. Our love would never dry up.

Time passes. As it does, it changes us, softens us, and matures us. And hopefully, by God's grace, enables us to see differently—correctly. That has certainly been true in the couple I just described.

What we perceived to be a "dried up" love was actually a depth of love we didn't know about yet or comprehend. This couple had a love for one another that included words but went beyond words. The other's presence was enough. Just to be together was sufficient. And to be in one another's presence, words or no words, was life-giving.

When we think about "making time" for God each day, or "carving out space," we often think of this as more of a discipline than a desire. Yet what we see in the life of Jesus, and in the lives of so many Christian women and men who have come before us, is that the spiritual life is marked by great desire.

Spending time with God is not so much a discipline as it is a desire.

This was true in the life of Jesus, whom Scripture tells us would get up early, sometimes before dawn, to meet with his Father (Mark 1:35). A time that was characterized certainly by words, but many times without them. To be in the presence of one you love is enough. And to be in the presence of the One who meets us, molds us, loves us, and changes us is vital to a life of love.

Sometimes, these solitary moments each day are filled with words. Humble and desperate prayers. Reading Scripture. Or just meditating on a verse. And other times, there is silence. Regardless, God's presence is enough, whether we are aware of his closeness and love or not.

> **Spending time with God is not so much a discipline as it is a desire.**

So, more than focusing on growing your discipline to make a consistent time each day with God a priority, focus on the desire. The longing we all feel to be put back together again, sustained and satisfied by him alone. We can take our heart to many different places, but the only place we can take our heart to be healed and strengthened is into God's presence.

Today, let's focus on moving from discipline to desire. How can we change the way we see our time alone with God? Let's begin by doing an honest assessment. Reflect on the following questions to better understand where you are.

Moving from Discipline to Desire

- In thinking about your time with God, how would *you* describe your relationship with him right now?
- In thinking about your time with God, how would *he* describe your relationship with him right now?
- If you could use one word to describe your desire to be alone with God each day, what would it be and why?
- Identify one temptation you face on a regular basis that threatens to turn your time with God into more of a discipline and less of a desire.

A key verse for today is Psalm 73:25. Slowly read and reread this verse, focusing primarily on the word *desire*. Once you have done this, reflect on the following questions:

- The process of desiring God above all things takes time! It is a lifelong process, so don't be discouraged. But what competing desires do you notice most often in your heart? For example, this could be the desire for comfort, approval, pleasure, etc.

- What is one desire you can ask the Holy Spirit to help you "crucify" to experience greater freedom and joy in Christ?

- Take a few minutes to honestly and humbly confess that to Jesus. Our first response should never be "I will try harder," but rather "Jesus, I need you." Rest in knowing that what we confess, Jesus meets with his grace.

- Finally, read 1 Thessalonians 5:17, where the apostle instructs us to "pray continually." How does this verse encourage us in the direction of seeing all of life as communion or friendship with God?

Take the next few moments to write out a prayer. Ask God to help you move from seeing your time with him as a discipline to more of a desire just to be with him. Be honest about where you are. And ask God to graciously give you more awareness of his presence.

• My Prayer •

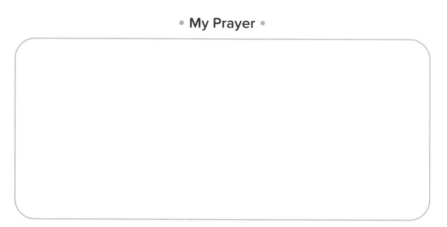

• Dig Deeper •

Read *Time for God* by Jacques Philippe.

• Highlighted Verse •

Whom have I in heaven but you?
And earth has nothing I desire besides you.

Psalm 73:25

Be the Boss of Your Screens

KAREN

I can tell you exactly where I was—and what I was doing—when I first laid eyes on what was known then as a smartphone. Some friends and I were out to dinner and one of them could hardly contain her enthusiasm because she had just purchased a first model iPhone. She excitedly claimed it was like having a computer in her hand! She could hop on the Internet, check her email when she wasn't by her computer, and could even take pictures with it. "Even when I am traveling or at home, it's like I've never left my office!" She seemed so pleased by this new development in technology. However, I remember my initial reaction being a bit cynical. I couldn't imagine why in the world I would want to check my email when I was at home or on vacation relaxing. It seemed rather intrusive. I honestly thought I'd pass on getting a smartphone and happily keep my old dumb one instead.

My, how times have changed! A decade and a half later, I am the owner of such a phone. And it does even more than that original version did, with apps for just about everything. People today are rarely without their phones within reach. So now, just about anyone who wants to reach us can—any time, and any place we are!

Modern technology can be a great tool. We can fall asleep faster listening to a sleep app with white noise (or my favorite, deep, smoothed brown noise). We can hop on social media and ask for prayer for a loved one who is ill. We can make our grocery list or determine whether our houseplant is dying from too much water or too little. However, there is a tender tipping point in our relationship with our devices. It is when our phones become the boss of us, rather than the other way around. They beep and buzz, sending us notifications of a new post on social media or a change in weather that is coming. They ding and ring, letting us know if someone has sent us a private message or is actually phoning us because they want to talk. If we let them, our phones can become tyrants, forcing us to pick up and respond, and dictating nearly our every move.

There has been much research done on how phone usage today is rewiring how we think, act, and interact with others. Experts say that even the presence of a phone when you are trying to have a face-to-face conversation with someone is disruptive. The other person fears that at any moment your phone might beckon you. When it does, you will suddenly choose it, elevating its significance over the importance of your conversation—thus even over your relationship with your friend.

> **The trivial becomes the adversary of the essential. We mindlessly tap, swipe, and scroll when we could be praying, studying, or connecting in real life with another living soul.**

Statistics tell us that the average person today reaches for their phone to check it, hop on an app, or send a text an average of 144 times a day. And they will spend roughly two hours and three minutes per day with their phones having their undivided attention. That adds up to fourteen hours per week![1] I wonder how many minutes of that fourteen hours is productive, crucial, or even useful and how much of it is trivial fluff?

You know the story. You think you're going to hop on the phone "real quick" just to check the latest news happenings on Twitter. Then, fifty minutes later, you are watching crazy squirrel videos or reading an in-depth article on the most popular shoe styles the year you were born. That is nearly an hour of your time you'll never get back!

If we want to live our priorities, we must carve out time for them. May I gently suggest that oodles of time can be found if we just learn to be the boss of our phones? (Please know that I'm preaching to myself here too!) Our phones can sometimes become an enemy from whom we need to be rescued. The trivial becomes the adversary of the essential. We mindlessly tap, swipe, and scroll when we could be praying, studying, or connecting in real life with another living soul.

Psalm 18 was written by David, most likely after the death of Saul, from whom he had been desperately fleeing. In it, he boldly speaks of God, who had granted him mercy, help, protection, and deliverance when he was being hunted. Psalm 18:17 declares, "He rescued me from my powerful enemy, from my foes, who were too strong for me." These words of David, describing his flight from a real human enemy, may be helpful for us today when we feel we are being hunted down relentlessly by the beeping and buzzing of our phones. Some of us are so tethered to our phones that we don't even realize we need rescuing. We get hits of dopamine, a neurotransmitter associated with our brain's pleasure and reward system. We become fixated on the constant information that parades before our eyes—or the even more addictive potential information we think may be just one more click away. (Did you know developers fashioned the "refresh" feature on apps to mimic the pull of a slot machine?!) This addictive pastime has us hooked. We need to be rescued. Then we can begin to put our phones in their proper place as a tool rather than a tyrant.

Here are some actions to ponder to help keep your phone from being the boss of you:

- Be brave. Check the amount of time you spent on your phone at the end of today by going into your settings and choosing "screen time." You may be shocked. However, the first step toward freedom is facing the truth. This stat will provide you with the accurate story.
- Identify your most likely times of day to mindlessly scroll. Is it on your lunch hour, when the kids are napping, or just before bed? Plan to turn your phone on silent (or do not disturb) during that time and choose a different task that is more important, like writing an encouraging note, reading a helpful book, or even doing a Bible study lesson.
- This one has greatly helped me: Consider treating your phone like an old-fashioned landline when you are at home. Keep it on the kitchen counter or an end table in the living area. Only use it in that location and do not carry it around with you.
- Have a friend hold you accountable (and maybe vice versa too!) with your screen time. At the end of the week, send her a screenshot of your total screen time. Knowing you have to report to someone may help keep the wasted time to a minimum.
- Make it a matter of prayer. Sincerely ask the Lord to convict you when you are wasting time on your devices. Ask him to give you the strength to put the screens away and use your time in a more productive or impactful manner.

Speaking of prayer, use the space below to pen a prayer, asking God to help you to not be at the mercy of your phone but to use it as a tool in life.

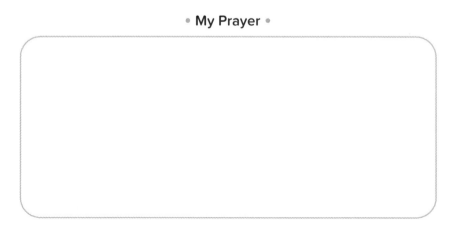

• My Prayer •

• **Dig Deeper** •

Listen to the *Made for This* podcast with Jennie Allen, "Bonus: How to Keep Technology from Running Your Life" with Andy Crouch.

A helpful app called SPACE: Break phone addiction, for both Android and IOS, is designed to help users manage their screen time and achieve digital balance.

• **Highlighted Verse** •

He rescued me from my powerful enemy, from my foes, who were too strong for me.

Psalm 18:17

day 9

Managing Your Responsibilities without Neglecting Your Relationships

KAREN

Not every one of us taking this forty-day quest lives the same life. One person may be a single Generation Z working woman, living in a city apartment while also taking online classes at night. Another may be a married and mothering millennial, at home full-time raising a few littles out in the suburbs, active in her community and church. There are empty nesters and first-time grandmas, those who care for aging parents, and others who care for their adorable fur babies. Our days look different; our responsibilities vary. But all of us have one thing in common: we are all navigating the tension between executing our responsibilities and tending to our relationships.

Yes. We all have people and we all have projects. One doesn't need to be employed outside of the home to have non-household work and responsibilities that must be taken care of. Many times our responsibilities and relationships collide, and we must make choices. We cannot lean toward either extreme: working hard at our many tasks while ignoring the people in our lives or letting the people in our lives dictate our every action so we end up neglecting our projects.

Having both relationships and responsibilities in our lives is not a problem to be solved; it is a tension we must manage, a balancing act that won't go away. We may have seasons when we don't have as many projects, so we have more time for people. At other times, we will be slammed with tasks, leaving little space for human interaction. However, for the most part, we will feel pressure from both aspects of life. How do we navigate life successfully, being attentive to both our work and our humans?

The book of Philippians is one of four letters the apostle Paul wrote from prison, likely near the end of his Roman imprisonment in AD 61 or 62. It is full of advice for finding joy despite trying circumstances. It also covers living in harmony with others by humbly emulating the behavior of Jesus. In the beginning of the second chapter, Paul urges, "Do not merely look out for your own personal interests, but also for the interests of others" (Philippians 2:4 AMP). It is a simple sentence, yet within it we see an important truth.

We can learn to strike a balance between our relationships and responsibilities— loving our people well without neglecting the duties God has called us to perform.

The verse does not say we should look out only for the interests of others, while neglecting our own. Nor does it say we need to make sure we are watching out for ourselves only and ignoring the interests of others. It states the obvious: we are going to have duties and activities that are in our interest and yet we need also to be mindful of the interests of others. The original Greek word translated into the phrase we read in English as "look out for" can offer us some insight.

This word, *skopeó* (pronounced *skop-eh'-o*) means to keep your eye on, to observe, to consider, or to contemplate. It also means to scrutinize carefully and then act. When it comes to our interests—tasks, duties, activities, and work—we would do well to keep a watchful eye on them to make sure they are getting done. However, we also must be mindfully observing the relationships in our lives, knowing that there will be times we are needed by others. It makes me think of wearing bifocals. Sometimes you are looking far away at what is happening in the distance. But often, you are focusing on what is right before you. Just as a person wearing such glasses must toggle between these two distances, we also need to toggle between our people and our projects. We can learn to strike a balance between our relationships and responsibilities—loving our people well without neglecting the duties God has called us to perform.

Answer the following questions as you scrutinize how you are doing at looking out for both your interests and the interests of others. Record your answers in the spaces provided.

- First, let's take inventory. Record the top five tasks you must accomplish each week. Use general categories such as your job, keeping up the household, tasks for a volunteer position, etc.

  1.

2.

3.

4.

5.

- Now list your top ten relationships you currently have. This may be immediate family, extended family, close friends, neighbors in need, someone from church, etc.

    1.

    2.

3.

4.

5.

6.

7.

8.

9.

10.

- Are there times when any of your tasks from the first list seem to be interrupted by someone on the second list who needs your attention? Briefly describe a situation where this happened.

- Looking back on that situation, how might it have been handled differently? Could you have been more direct with the person, letting them know you would happily talk with them or help them, but you needed an hour to finish your work first? Or, might you have placed your task on the back burner while you focused your attention on the person who was before you? Describe how you could have taken a different approach.

Oftentimes, we let others set our agendas because we get caught up pleasing people and fail to place boundaries. A boundary is something tangible and clearly communicated to another so they know what behavior to expect from you. For example, let's say you have a friend who constantly seems to call you on her drive home from work to process the drama going on in her life. However, that drive home comes during the time you are making and serving dinner to your family. A clear boundary in this case might be that you tell your friend you have made a policy to put your phone in the "do not disturb" mode during the supper hour so it will only allow calls from your immediate family members. This boundary is not cruel. Having such a practice does not mean you won't talk to her at another time that is convenient for both of you. A boundary in this case is actually loving because she will understand that it is nothing personal; you are just busy during the hour she is driving home and therefore unavailable to talk.

- Now it is your turn. Think of a situation where you would benefit from making and communicating a boundary to a person or persons in your life who tend to interrupt your work with things that are not important or serious. Write that boundary in the space below. Make sure to relay this boundary to the people it will affect. Then, follow through and implement it in your life.

- On the other side of the coin, do you ever tend to not be attentive in a relationship because you are too busy working? Maybe you are a young mother who wants so badly for the house to be all picked up before bedtime, but those little eyes are staring up at you, wanting a bedtime story read to them. Make a "principle when dealing with people" statement that articulates how you will handle this recurring situation. In the example given, the statement might be, "When my child clearly needs some love and attention from me, I will remind myself that I can always pick up the house later, once I've spent a few minutes with them." Write out any statement below that is unique to your own situation.

Using Philippians 2:4 as a springboard, craft a prayer about looking out for the interests of others while you also tend to the interests of your own life. Ask the Father to grant you discernment for how you should behave when a relationship and a responsibility seem to clash.

• My Prayer •

• Dig Deeper •

Listen to the *SHE* podcast with Jordan Lee Dooley, "A Framework for Finding Work-Life Balance" featuring Tina Wells.

• Highlighted Verse •

Do not merely look out for your own personal interests, but also for the interests of others.

Philippians 2:4 AMP

day 10

How to Stick to
the Priorities You Set

RUTH

Priorities are easy enough to understand. Hopefully, by now you have an even greater grasp on what is a priority to you, given your season and set of circumstances in life. So, knowing what are the most important things we are to give our time and attention to each day, the real challenge is actually sticking to those priorities!

What are those priorities for you? What are the things you have set apart from all the other daily to-dos and rhythms, things that you want to give yourself more fully to? And then, of course, how do you stick to those priorities?

The Bible gives a rather simple answer to sticking to our priorities. It might sound odd, but sticking to your priorities requires, well, *sticking to your priorities!* Quite simply, it is not terribly popular. In one word, the secret is perseverance. Perseverance is sticking with something or someone even when it is hard.

The New Testament is full of exhortations to persevere and endure. For example, we read in Hebrews 10:36, "You need to persevere so that when you have done the will of God, you will receive what he has promised." And in James 1:12, we're told what those who stick with Jesus will receive someday: "Blessed is the one who perseveres under trial because, having stood the test, that person will receive the crown of life that the Lord has promised to those who love him."

We are called to persevere in following Jesus.
Persevere while we wait for his return.
In trials and suffering, we endure.
We are to keep giving ourselves to what matters most.

We are called not to enthusiasm, but to endurance. Enthusiasm comes and goes. The real test for every follower of Jesus is persevering when it is hard.

There is always a reward for not giving up. We can't always see the fruit of our labor. Our faithfulness can seem fuzzy—or at least the outcomes of our faithfulness. We don't always know what God is going to do or how he is going to honor our obedience, but he always does. Persevering is worth it!

I love the words of Fulton Sheen on this theme of perseverance. He once wrote, "Decisions and resolutions taken during an enthusiastic moment meant little unless tested by time and waiting." Then he adds, "It is always a good policy never to choose the most enthusiastic person in a gathering as a leader. Wait to see how much wood there is for the flame."[1]

> We are called not to enthusiasm, but to endurance.

What does all that have to do with sticking with your priorities? It's okay to be excited about those goals or dreams or priorities you set. But the real challenge is to persevere—adhering to those priorities even when it is hard.

So if you have identified what your priorities are, don't give up when you fall short. Don't despair or throw in the towel if you don't follow through every single time. Get up! Begin again, right where you are, and with God's help, keep going. Stick with what you feel God has called you to in this season. Pray that you would not be dry wood rapidly consumed by the fire.

Today, let's take a closer look at the difference between enthusiasm and endurance. Take some time to prayerfully think through and answer the following questions.

Enthusiasm and Endurance

- Describe a time when you were enthusiastic about something, but failed to endure.

- Why is it important to make a distinction between enthusiasm and endurance?

- What does perseverance or endurance prove in the life of a Christian?

- How is God calling you to grow in perseverance?

- Think again about Hebrews 10:36. In it, the writer is encouraging Christians to persevere in their faithfulness to Jesus. Prayerfully read this verse and reflect on the following questions:

  » What does the writer connect perseverance to?

  » Why is doing the "will of God" so critical to growing in perseverance?

» What is the promise the writer is speaking of?

» As you apply this theme of perseverance to your own priorities, what is most important for you to keep in mind each day?

Take the next few moments to record a prayer asking for God's grace to endure. Pray that, through the Holy Spirit, he would guide you into greater faithfulness to his will in this season of your life.

• My Prayer •

• Dig Deeper •

Read *Leaders Who Last* by Dave Kraft.

• Highlighted Verse •

You need to persevere so that when you have done the will of God, you will receive what he has promised.

Hebrews 10:36

Finding the Proper Perspective

To live your priorities, you must possess the proper perspective on the various components that make up your life—your work, your relationships, your responsibilities in the home, and the reality of your need for times of rest. These next ten days will help you to explore gaining this proper perspective and discovering how the various moving parts of your relationships and responsibilities can work together. The exercises provided and the reflection questions given will help you unearth truths in Scripture that will shape your perspective and therefore begin to shape your habits as well.

This Is What's Standing in the Way of Your Progress

KAREN

When my children were young, they simply adored our daily read-out-loud times in the afternoon before any little ones who needed a nap went to sleep. Perhaps the most loved books were the ones about life on the prairie penned by Laura Ingalls Wilder. Our oldest son especially grew fond of anything having to do with the exploration of uncharted territory by early American settlers. His dream was to one day ride on an old covered wagon.

I made it a habit to lead my kids in researching concepts or historical happenings about which they were curious. So we trekked off to the library to gather info about ordinary families traveling in covered wagons. Did you know that today there are nearly a dozen places—from Missouri to Idaho to Oregon, and more—where you can still see the indentations made by wagon wheels? Those pioneering buggies forged a trail for thousands of settlers to travel upon, made when wagon wheels from all the vehicles repeatedly traversed over the same spot in the soil decade after decade. Soon the grass died, and a hard, compact dirt road emerged. The repetitive motion of the wooden wagon wheels made for a permanent path.

Brain experts assert that our mind works in much the same way. It is called rumination. *Mind Diagnostics* describes rumination as "a pattern of excessive, obsessive, and repetitive thinking of negative events, concepts, or outcomes from the past that is not traditionally solution-oriented, and for many people, it persists regardless of external stimulus confirming or denying the validity of the negative thought process."[1] Rumination has us replaying past events, choices, and situations over and over in our mind. This can make us feel trapped. We are nearly doomed to repeat the same behavior because we let our minds wander down the same paths they have traveled down dozens of times in the past.

Such reoccurring thought patterns can sabotage our productivity. When our mind takes a familiar path, our thoughts almost always come to the same conclusion. For example, if we have longed to be diligent about rising early to spend some time alone with God—but rarely see it happen—our minds might have a repeated thought pattern similar to this: "I am a Christian. Good Christians get up early to read the Bible and pray. I want to be a good Christian, so I should do the same thing. However, I just can't seem to drag myself out of bed when the early alarm goes off. I just keep hitting snooze. I'm too tired and just want to sleep, so I don't get up to meet with Jesus. I am such a failure. Maybe I'll never be spiritually disciplined like other successful Christians are."

> **We desperately need to renew our minds. Thankfully, our Creator—who made us and knows this about us—provides a way for us to do just that.**

These negative narratives can impair our progress because they keep us stuck in the past where a positive outcome was not obtained. They paralyze us, keeping us from moving ahead, forming new thought patterns, and as a result, new actions. We desperately need to renew our minds. Thankfully, our Creator—who made us and knows this about us—provides a way for us to do just that.

Romans 12:2 CSB commands us, "Do not be conformed to this age, but be transformed by the renewing of your mind, so that you may discern what is the good, pleasing, and perfect will of God." The original Greek word translated into English as "renewing" is *anakainósis* (pronounced *an-ak-ah'-ee-no-sis*). It means to experience a complete change of heart and life, to make fresh; it is a brand-new development, or a regeneration made possible by God's power. This Greek word is used only twice in the New Testament: here in Romans 12:2, and in Titus 3:5 where it states, "he saved us—not by works of righteousness that we had done, but according to his mercy—through the washing of regeneration and renewal by the Holy Spirit" (CSB).

Such regeneration and renewal of our mind comes from the Father and is empowered through the Holy Spirit. We are told that the renewing of our mind will make us transformed. This Greek word *metamorphoó* (pronounced *met-am-or-fo'-o*) might look and sound familiar to you. It is very similar to our English word *metamorphosis*. This term undoubtedly reminds you of the transformation of a simple caterpillar into a beautiful butterfly. The change is utterly astonishing, as a colorful and stunning butterfly is substantially different from a green, worm-like creature. This is what can happen to our mind when we allow the Lord—through the power of the Spirit—to renew it.

Here are some tips for allowing God to renew your mind. The foundation of this is prayer. In prayer alone to God, converse with him about the following:

- The reality that God's thoughts are different from ours. Isaiah 55:8–9 csb declares, "'For my thoughts are not your thoughts, and your ways are not my ways.' This is the Lord's declaration. 'For as heaven is higher than earth, so my ways are higher than your ways, and my thoughts than your thoughts.'" God can only think the truth. We, on the other hand, can easily let our minds become riveted on incorrect beliefs and negative notions. Begin by thanking God for his pure and true thoughts toward you. Ask him to allow your thoughts to come into alignment with his.

- Realize that God has granted us understanding. Scripture tells us in 1 John 5:20 csb, "And we know that the Son of God has come and has given us understanding so that we may know the true one. We are in the true one—that is, in his Son, Jesus Christ. He is the true God and eternal life." If you belong to Jesus, you know the ultimate truth—Jesus himself. Jesus came and has given us understanding to know God. When we know God, we can trust what he says about us: that we are chosen, treasured, and greatly loved.

    Look up the following verses. In the space provided after each, jot what you learn about what God thinks of you.

1 Peter 2:9

Ephesians 1:4

John 15:16

Ephesians 2:17–22

Romans 8:28–29

- How can knowing what God thinks of you prevent you from fall-ing back into old, well-worn thought patterns about yourself, your abilities (or disabilities), or your goals in life? Take a few moments to think about a negative groove your mind seems to fall into re-peatedly. Write it out below. Then write out the truth of what God thinks about that situation. Use any Scripture references that may back up what you write.

My negative thoughts groove:

The truth about what God thinks:

Scriptures that back this up:

Isaiah 43:18–19 reads, "'Forget the former things; do not dwell on the past. See, I am doing a new thing! Now it springs up; do you not perceive it? I am making a way in the wilderness and streams in the wasteland.'"

Isaiah's depiction of a faithful God who would provide a way forward for Israel helped highlight the truth that a holy and omnipotent God would enable them to live lives of obedience that would ultimately provide a way and sustenance for them in the future. *The Moody Bible Commentary* explains, "It inspires them not to accept that which appears to be prudent, rational, or expedient, but to think with a theological rationale that calls them to trust in God to intervene, to protect, and to rule."[2] Although the words in this passage were meant originally for the people in Isaiah's time, they can be a reminder to us that the same God who made a way back then is still in the business of making ways today. He provided the way of salvation through his son, Jesus Christ. And God can provide a way for us to move forward in the renewal of our mind, trusting the Holy Spirit to help our thinking to align with Scripture. We aren't facing a literal desert or rough terrain, but we sometimes feel as if our way in life is emotionally or spiritually rough, so we stay trapped in the same mindset that keeps us from changing our actions and moving forward.

Using what you have read today, create a prayer in the space below, asking God to help you not to stay stuck in the ruts of the past, but to renew your mind and to live your life confidently in Christ.

• My Prayer •

• Dig Deeper •

Read *Renewing Your Mind: Become More Like Christ* by Neil T. Anderson. Listen to the *Passion + Purpose* podcast with Louie Giglio, Season 1, episode 9: "How to Reduce Anxiety and Renew Your Mind" with Dr. Caroline Leaf.

• Highlighted Verse •

Do not be conformed to this age, but be transformed by the renewing of your mind, so that you may discern what is the good, pleasing, and perfect will of God.

Romans 12:2 CSB

day 12

The Danger of Sacrificing the Things That Matter Most

RUTH

What matters most to you? Or maybe, asked another way, what does success look like to you? We all have different visions of what we think "the good life" is. And our culture is certainly not short on ways it tries to convince us of what to chase!

So if we are going to experience a life that we actually love, we have to pursue what matters most—what really matters to God. If we are not careful, we can chase the wrong things, sacrificing what matters most, or matters more, along the way. That danger is real.

Stephen Covey sums up this potential pitfall so clearly, with his sobering reminder that what we chase matters:

> It's incredibly easy to get caught up in an activity trap, in the busy-ness of life, to work harder and harder at climbing the ladder of success only to discover it's leaning against the wrong wall.[1]

Imagine a person who spends his or her entire life chasing wealth or material possessions. They think that if they just have more, or something nicer and new, they will be happy. That is success, they claim. Or imagine a person who spends their whole life pursuing the approval of someone they look up to or admire. And once they do get the approval, they discover that they feel just as empty as they did before. Imagine the person who thinks that what matters is another experience—one more trip or vacation. More pleasure. And yet, years down the road, they discover "one more" will never be enough. These are just some of the examples of people who have been leaning a ladder against the wrong wall.

In Mark 8:34, Jesus begins to describe what it looks like to follow him— what it means to be his true disciple. At the heart of being a follower of Jesus is learning to die to ourselves and live for God. It's actually in losing our life that we find our life, Jesus is teaching. It is in this context that Jesus gives a warning—again, a sobering reminder that there is always something that gets sacrificed when we are running after the wrong thing. Jesus asks, "What good is it for someone to gain the whole world, yet forfeit their soul?" (Mark 8:36).

Our lives follow what we love.

People achieve "success" every single day. But there is always a cost. Success always comes with a sacrifice. Sometimes people sacrifice their health to achieve their vision of success. They work long hours. Because of how busy they are, or think they are, they fail to eat what is healthy. They might not take good care of their body in other respects. And while they might get what they want, it eventually costs them their health in some way.

Others will sacrifice important relationships (family and friends) to "gain the world." Little or no time is spent getting together or going out. Phone calls and text messages—let alone time spent face-to-face—no longer exist. Relationships, building community, or serving the needs of others is of little or no value.

Some people sacrifice the most important relationship—an intimate friendship with God. Pursuing their vision of the good life, they do not cultivate a vibrant or real faith. The church is of no value to them. We might say the eternal gets sacrificed for the earthly.

We can all be in danger of sacrificing for success the things that really matter to God. It can be easy or tempting to lose sight of what counts or will count for eternity. So today, as you reflect upon your own life and priorities, be honest before God about what matters most to you. Take some time to reflect on the following questions. Ask God to give you the grace to see what is important in his eyes.

Assessing What We Love

- Our lives follow what we love. What would you say has become more important to you than loving God and loving others?

- If someone were to evaluate your financial spending, what would they conclude about the things you are investing in?

- If someone were to evaluate your time, what would they conclude you really value?

- If someone were to evaluate your relationships with family or friends, what observations do you think they would make?

A key passage for today is Mark 8:34–36. Jesus is talking about what it looks like to follow him. He is always honest about the cost of being his disciple. He wants us to beware of giving ourselves to the wrong things. Read this passage in that context and prayerfully ask the Holy Spirit to speak to you. Once you have done this, reflect on the following questions:

- What needs to be crucified in your own life to follow Jesus more fully?

- What are ways that you try to "gain the whole world"?

- What are you sacrificing right now that you shouldn't be? Is it a re-lationship, your health, rest, a deeper friendship with God?

- Identify one or two things you can begin to do differently so you are no longer sacrificing what matters most.

Take the next few moments to write out a prayer. Ask God to give you discernment. Create a prayer of commitment or renewal confessing any areas of your life that have become more important than your walk with God.

• My Prayer •

• Dig Deeper •

Read *Counterfeit Gods: The Empty Promises of Money, Sex, and Power, and the Only Hope that Matters* by Timothy Keller.

• Highlighted Verse •

What good is it for someone to gain the whole world, yet forfeit their soul?

Mark 8:36

day 13

Why Finding Time for Yourself Today Will Make All the Difference Tomorrow

RUTH

I know it might sound selfish, but you need to make time for YOU each day—or as close to each day as you can! Because when we do this today, God gives us the strength to love him and others as we should tomorrow. If we are spent today, we'll be in no shape to love and serve tomorrow.

No matter what season of life you are in or what circumstances you are walking through, God wants to meet with you. And making time for you requires that you have a biblical understanding of *you*. In other words, it is helpful here to just say a few things about who we are as human beings made in the image and likeness of God (Genesis 1:26–27).

The Bible teaches that we are body, soul, and spirit. We might say we are material beings called into a relationship with an immaterial God! We are made from the stuff of earth (Genesis 2:7, 21–22) and yet God breathes his breath into us, making us living beings. In Romans 8:11 we are reminded that our bodies matter in the spiritual life and are/will be renewed by the Holy Spirit. The apostle Paul writes, "And if the Spirit of him who raised Jesus from the dead is living in you, he who raised Christ from the dead will also give life to your *mortal bodies* because of his Spirit who lives in you" (emphasis added). Perhaps most specific and detailed are Paul's words about our resurrected bodies (1 Corinthians 15:35–58). Our earthly bodies have a future—we will have a resurrected body, like Jesus. The body is good! So it matters how we take care of it.

But we have a spiritual side too. We are created with the capacity to know and love God. We are not just physical beings. And we're not souls trapped in a body. The Christian faith, from its earliest days, has taught that the human person is body and soul.

So what does all this have to do with making time for you? A lot! If we want to feel refreshed and recharged by God's grace, we need to pay attention to the *whole* person—body and soul. This might mean that when we carve out time each day, we need to focus on some of the following:

- Getting good-quality and adequate rest
- Exercising
- Eating healthy foods
- Addressing any physical causes for feelings of anxiety, prolonged sadness, lack of energy, etc.
- Taking good care of our bodies—doing our best to walk in good health or walk through health issues that are out of our control
- And of course, continuing to make time to read, pray, meditate on Scripture, and stay engaged in God-honoring community

All these practices can and do recharge you—the whole you. In a passage of Scripture we'll look at in the following section, we are reminded that the Christian life is lived out in the body. As you think about all that is happening in your life right now, it is important to keep in mind the different ways God wants you to take care of yourself—body and soul. These disciplines, or practices, are not meant primarily for us. We are called to take care of ourselves so that ultimately, we might be able to live out the greatest commandment—which is to love God and love others. So don't forget that self-care is not selfish if properly understood. It should lead to greater selfless care for others!

> **If we are spent today, we'll be in no shape to love and serve tomorrow.**

Today, let's take some time to focus on how you are doing. Again, when I say *you*, I am referring to all of you—the whole you, body and soul. Prayerfully consider some of the following questions to get a better understanding of where you are at and what you need most right now to walk in greater love for God and others by first taking care of yourself.

The Whole You

- How would you describe your spiritual life right now and why?

- How would you describe your physical life right now and why?

- What depletes you most spiritually?

- What depletes you most physically?

- Are there one or two things you know you need to do to take better care of yourself either spiritually or physically right now?

To help us understand today's topic, let's read Romans 6:11–14. Here, the apostle Paul is talking about the role our bodies play in our spiritual lives. Our bodies matter, and they are the place where our faith is lived out. (See also Galatians 2:20.) Prayerfully read and reread these verses. Once you have done this, reflect on the following questions:

- How would you describe the role our bodies play in following Jesus?

- Prayerfully take a body scan and ask the Holy Spirit to show you where sin has a hold on you.

- What "evil desires" do you need to identify and allow the Holy Spirit to heal and correct?

- What are one or two practical ways you can take this week to care for *you* so that you can love others well tomorrow?

Take the next few moments to write out a prayer. Ask God to strengthen you and bring new life to your body and soul. Confess any sin that you are made aware of and ask for God's grace to walk in greater obedience.

• My Prayer •

• Dig Deeper •

Listen to the *Get Your Hopes Up* podcast with Christy Wright, Season 1, episode 27: "The Type of Rest You're Missing Out On."

Listen to the *Made for This* podcast with Jennie Allen, "Does God Care about Our Bodies?" December 20, 2022.

• Highlighted Verse •

And if the Spirit of him who raised Jesus from the dead is living in you, he who raised Christ from the dead will also give life to your mortal bodies because of his Spirit who lives in you.

Romans 8:11

Why Multitasking Is Killing Your Progress

KAREN

When I was in college, each month our dorm floor held a meeting where an older woman from campus, such as a professor or administrative faculty member, gave a lecture on achieving success in some aspect of life. The topic might be on spiritual growth or career success. Oftentimes it was about how to succeed at the everyday tasks of life we would face once we left campus and officially began adulting. Whatever the topic, we munched on chips and salsa—or popcorn made in my trusty air popper—and listened intently, hoping to learn something that would benefit us in the future.

One of these casual but informative lectures still stands out in my mind. It was delivered by a professor who was also married to the dean of students. She was deeply involved in church life and acted as an advisor to one of the sports groups on campus. She seemed like a bright and industrious woman who was able to get many tasks done simultaneously. As she spoke, she briefly covered the topic of productivity. When one of my floormates asked her how she was able to accomplish so much in both life and work, she offered a simple sentence as her secret: "I've just learned to be really, *really* good at multitasking."

As a senior who was soon to head out into the world, I tucked her little statement away in my brain, surmising it would help me to also be industrious, checking off multiple accomplishments on my long to-do list each day. Being busy was almost a badge of honor to me. In fact, I remember catching a clip of Oprah Winfrey on television at that time saying that her goal was to be so busy she couldn't breathe. To me, that was what success looked like. You took on multiple tasks and simultaneously juggled them like a seasoned circus pro. And—here's the kicker—you could keep all the plates spinning without dropping a single one.

Now, with a few decades under my belt as an adult, I realize something: multitasking is a myth. Oh, we might *think* we are doing two or three things at once, but in reality, our brain is constantly toggling between actions, tasks, devices, information we are listening to or watching—you name it! Author Carey Lohrenz put it this way:

> What we're really doing when we multitask is *switching back and forth* between two or more objects of our attention—we're *task switching*. Often, there's little rhyme or reason for the switching. That's especially the case when we let little distractions and ongoing worries interrupt our focus. When we're task switching, we aren't fully engaged in anything.[1]

How true! And how much task switching has increased as the world has grown older. In my mom's day, she might've tried folding the laundry while talking on the landline phone and also trying to follow along with the news playing in the background on the television set. However, today we have even more tasks and objects vying for our attention—especially screens. In fact, it's not uncommon for someone to have three device screens before them at home as they are working. The television might be on while a laptop is balanced on your knees, and a phone is in one hand because a text just came in. This is in addition to whatever—or whomever—is also competing for your focus.

Multitasking is not only a myth, but it can also derail our productivity. All this task toggling doesn't help us get things done more quickly. Quite the opposite! It makes responsibilities take longer.

You may be surprised to learn that experts claim "toggling back and forth between tasks—even just taking thirty seconds to send a text—slows us down and can even derail your mental ability *for up to a full half hour* afterward!"[2] I certainly see this when I am trying to write something for a book or magazine. If I am not intentional in drowning out any distractions that come my way—a notification on my computer or the buzz of my phone—I get slowed down significantly. When I stop to "just check my Instagram messages real quick" or read a text from someone, my brain cannot jump right back into the groove, picking up creatively where I left off. No. Now I must reread what I was writing before the interruption came to get the flow going again.

> **We must remember that we are serving the Lord no matter the task at hand. If we want to work from the soul, putting in our very best effort, we need to nix the multitasking and zero in and be present, concentrating on one task—or one person—at a time.**

I love the words of the apostle Paul in Colossians 3:23–24 where he urges the believers in Colossae to think about how they work. The Amplified version of the Bible describes it thoroughly: "Whatever you do [whatever your task may be], work from the soul [that is, put in your very best effort], as [something done] for the Lord and not for men, knowing [with all certainty] that it is from the Lord [not from men] that you will receive the inheritance which is your [greatest] reward. It is the Lord Christ whom you [actually] serve." We must remember that we are serving the Lord no matter the task at hand. If we want to work from the soul, putting in our very best effort, we need to nix the multitasking and zero in and be present, concentrating on one task—or one person—at a time.

To help gain more focus, let's give ourselves a little assessment on this multitasking mayhem.

- On a scale of one to ten—with one being horrible and ten being fantastic—how would you rate yourself on how often you are distracted by trying to multitask.

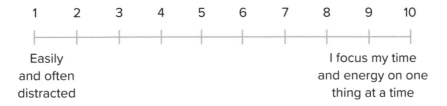

- What duties, chores, and responsibilities do you tend to combine? List them below. Then write why this is detrimental to your quest to do each of these things well. How has multitasking actually hurt your productivity and labor excellence?

- How do the words of Colossians 3:23–24 inspire you? Do you think of your daily tasks as being done for Jesus himself? If you kept that in mind, how might this change how you attack your work each day?

Using Paul's words in Colossians 3:23–24 as a springboard, craft a prayer to God about your productivity and your desire to focus whole-heartedly on the task at hand, without being distracted by the allure of the myth of multitasking.

• My Prayer •

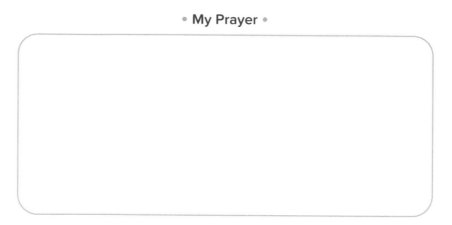

• Dig Deeper •

Read *She Works His Way: A Practical Guide for Doing What Matters Most in a Get-Things-Done World* by Michelle Myers and Somer Phoebus.

A handy app, Todoist: To-Do List & Planner, helps you plan your work and focus on only the matter at hand.

• Highlighted Verses •

Whatever you do [whatever your task may be], work from the soul [that is, put in your very best effort], as [something done] for the Lord and not for men, knowing [with all certainty] that it is from the Lord [not from men] that you will receive the inheritance which is your [greatest] reward. It is the Lord Christ whom you [actually] serve.

Colossians 3:23–24 AMP

day 15

You Can't Be Friends with Everyone

RUTH

"How about coffee sometime?"

"We'd love to have you and your family over for dinner!"

"Would you want to start meeting each week and walking together?"

I'm sure you can think of your own list of questions or requests—all sincere and good. I am so grateful for the many friends God has placed in my life through the years. I am always amazed when I think about God's goodness in giving friends, for different reasons, in different seasons. And, of course, I am grateful for the opportunities I have had to be that kind of friend to others over the years.

But we probably all can admit that certain seasons bring about new limitations. Friends are no exception. As much as we love people and are on the receiving end of other people's love, we come to the realization that we just can't be friends with everyone. Which is really hard for someone like me who is an extrovert! Even if we *want* to be friends with everyone, we eventually discover that we *can't* be friends with everyone.

The challenge becomes discerning who we can, or should, enter into deeper friendship with. Understanding the real dynamics of limited time and energy, season of life, availability, and current responsibilities, we are forced to choose wisely if we are to actually experience a life we love.

It reminds me of an illustration Henri Nouwen used in his book *The Inner Voice of Love.* He describes our interior world—we might say our heart—as a castle surrounded by a moat. Envision a castle surrounded by water, with those inside lowering and raising its drawbridge. The drawbridge, when it is down, gives access to anyone and everyone. But the castle, when its drawbridge is raised, protects the access. No entry is available.

That castle with its drawbridge, explains Nouwen, is like the access we give others. He writes, "For years you have permitted others to walk in and out of your life according to their needs and desires. Thus, you were no longer the master in your own house,"[1] What a powerful illustration of how boundaries with friends are necessary to keep us together and not just keep others out.

> **Coming to the realization that you can't be friends with everyone is not permission to avoid being friends with anyone.**

I think of the classic example of deep and meaningful friendship in the biblical example of Jonathan and David. It was marked by a mutual self-giving love for one another. There was need without neediness. Depth without demands.

A healthy friendship is one marked by mutual self-giving. And like Jonathan and David's, it is rooted in the love of God. It is safe and secure. Not overly high-maintenance, because as friends, we know we are not gods to one another. Our deepest thirst and hunger is, first and foremost, satisfied in Christ.

We read an important detail about their friendship in 1 Samuel 23:16 that shows this. David's needs were real. He was being pursued by King Saul. So David, running for his life, flees into the desert. But it is in the desert where David is refreshed by his friend Jonathan. We read, "And Saul's son Jonathan went to David at Horesh and *helped him find strength in God*" (emphasis added).

Who are those friends who find you in your own desert? Who are those friends who need you to wander into their wilderness, and walk with them? Coming to the realization that you can't be friends with *everyone* is not permission to avoid being friends with *anyone*. Rather, with wisdom, we need to discern those friendships that will help us "find strength in God." We need to cultivate those friendships that lead us both closer to the heart of God.

Today, let's examine how we can make those choices to be friends with some without the burden of feeling like we have to be friends with all.

Raising the Drawbridge

- What are the most important friendships in your life right now and why?

- What motivates your desire for friendships—the desire to love or the desire to be loved?

- If you were to pull back from certain friendships, which would those be and why?

- What is the difference between loving someone deeply and loving them freely?

Let's look today at Mark 3:13. Before Jesus sends his disciples out, he calls those "he wanted." They were with him. Not just a mission but true friendship existed between Jesus and his disciples. Take some time to read Mark 3:13, considering the theme of being with others. Once you have done this, reflect on the following:

- Pray about who Jesus is calling you into deeper friendship with. Identify two or three people you want to intentionally develop closer friendships with.
- What does it look like to be thankful for what a friend *can* give you instead of thinking about what they *should* give you?
- What is one way today that you can help a friend "find strength in God"?
- And finally, in what specific ways can you protect your heart from friends who want to enter your life for their needs only?

Take the next few moments to write out a prayer. Ask God to give you wisdom, compassion, and courage. Ask the Lord to help you to be a Christlike friend, but also show you how to build Christlike friendships.

• My Prayer •

• Dig Deeper •

Read *Relationships: A Mess Worth Making* by Timothy S. Lane and Paul David Tripp.

• Highlighted Verse •

And Saul's son Jonathan went to David at Horesh and helped him find strength in God.

1 Samuel 23:16

The First Sunday Secret for a Productive and Peaceful Week

KAREN

Do you dread Mondays? You know, that recurring initial weekday that kicks off yet another multiday stretch of crazy—where you attempt to juggle accomplishing all your work responsibilities and managing your many relationships while also keeping things running smoothly around your house? Just the thought of another Monday can make me start to hyperventilate ever so slightly. However, I have learned the importance of two simple words that help to make my week productive and peaceful *if* I turn my attention to these two words every Sunday. They are *rest* and *routine*. We will cover these concepts over two days. First, let's explore rest—or more precisely, the lack thereof.

The concept of resting on Sundays has been around for ages. The Jewish people rested on the Sabbath—the seventh day of the week, which is Saturday—ceasing their work as was decreed in the Old Testament in the ten commandments (Exodus 20:8). After the coming of Jesus and the birth of the Christian church, in Acts 20:7, we see Paul speaking of meeting with the believers in Ephesus on the first day of the week to break bread together. In 1 Corinthians 16:1–2, the church in Corinth was told to take up a collection on the first day of the week, which seems to indicate that was their meeting day. And Roman history reveals that the church was in the habit of meeting on Sunday very soon after the death of the apostles. Many biblical scholars think this is because Jesus rose from the dead on the first day of the week. Thus, the early Christians went from observing a Saturday Sabbath to observing what was called the Lord's Day on Sunday. The early American Puritans believed the command about the Sabbath carried over to the observance of the Lord's Day, so they refrained from working on Sundays unless it was for necessity, charity, or something that pertained to worship. Even at my Christian college, we were discouraged from doing any work on Sundays, including homework.

> **We don't rest because we've earned it, having worked hard all week. We rest to be more effectively productive in the days ahead because we've been spiritually rejuvenated.**

The concept of a Sabbath rest has become crucial to me. However, it might not be in the way you'd think—as a reward for six days of productivity. We don't rest because we've earned it, having worked hard all week. We rest to be more effectively productive in the days ahead because we've been spiritually rejuvenated. And Sundays provide the perfect opportunity for rest, breaking from our normal pattern of work so we can be refreshed. (I know not everyone can do this on Sundays. The point is to have one day a week when you can observe some Sabbath time.)

In Mark 6:31 CSB we find Jesus' instruction to "'Come away by yourselves to a remote place and rest for a while.' For many people were coming and going, and they did not even have time to eat." Our Lord longed for his disciples to pull away from the busyness of everyday life and experience rest. It is just as imperative that we, as his disciples today, do the same. I find it interesting that the original Greek word translated to English as "away" doesn't just mean to go to a new location. It also means against or opposite. Isn't that telling? For us to pull away and rest for a while goes against our current culture. It is the opposite behavior we are accustomed to displaying. It might not only feel countercultural to implement a weekly time of rest— we might find we are also fighting against ourselves! But it is imperative that we work in a period of rejuvenation that will help to reset our brains and refocus our energies as it refreshes us spiritually.

Here is what rest looks like for me weekly. (Note: I am showing you my routine as an example, not as something to replicate. Use the journaling sections for today and tomorrow to prayerfully consider how you can create a routine that allows you to experience rest.)

- I do my best to prepare ahead so I can experience a restful Sunday. This means thinking about Sunday supper a day or two ahead. I may prepare a meatloaf and a side dish on Saturday, along with a tossed salad and dessert. Then on Sunday, I just need to toss things in the oven, dress the salad, and dinner is served. I work ahead to have the laundry done, the house relatively clean and clutter-free, and anything else buttoned up so I won't have these tasks to do Sunday.

- I have a practice of not creating anything on Sundays. Since I am a content creator—writing for books, blogs, magazines, and social media posts—I break from my normal routine by not doing any of this on Sunday. What constitutes work for you will be different, but consider taking a break from it one day a week.
- The Puritans used to assert that the Sabbath was not for carnal rest, meaning sleeping. I think they were sorely mistaken! When you work hard all week, taking a Sunday afternoon nap—without setting the alarm—is a real treat. I do it almost every week.
- I also try to enjoy at least one activity that I find restful. This might be sitting in a chaise lawn chair reading a novel in the summer sunshine. It might be taking a walk on some local trails and admiring the brightly colored fall foliage. Or it may be curling up under a blanket in front of the fireplace and watching a historical documentary in the winter.
- I put my phone in "do not disturb" mode for the entire day. This only allows calls and texts from my immediate family members. I also stay off social media, with very few exceptions. (One friend even deletes those apps from her phone and reinstalls them Monday morning!)

Now it is your turn. Grab something to drink and spend some uninterrupted time working your way through the questions below to find your own weekly rhythm of rest.

- First, think about which day would be the best for you to implement as a Sabbath day of rest. Will it be Sunday? Another day? Or will it vary from week to week due to your ever-changing work schedule? Write the day or plan below.

- How will you build in time to rest? What can you do ahead of time so you can do less on your Sabbath?

- What activities that relax and rejuvenate you will you try to work into your Sabbath day? List any below.

- Can you take time for a nap? (I know that isn't always easy when there are young children around. You might need to get clever. When my kids were old enough, I would sometimes allow them to have a snack and watch an approved movie while I snoozed in the recliner nearby!)

Finally, using Mark 6:31 as a springboard, create a prayer in the space provided below, asking God to help you carve out a regular time of rest and spiritual rejuvenation each week.

• My Prayer •

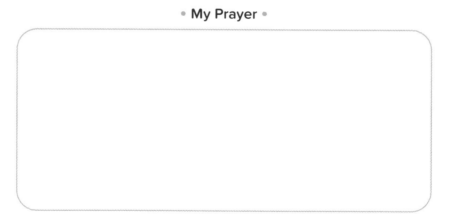

• Dig Deeper •

Listen to the *Daily Grace* podcast, episode 192: "What the Bible Says About Physical and Spiritual Rest."

• Highlighted Verse •

He said to them, "Come away by yourselves to a remote place and rest for a while." For many people were coming and going, and they did not even have time to eat.

Mark 6:31 CSB

day 17

The Second Sunday Secret for a Productive and Peaceful Week

KAREN

In the previous entry, we looked at the first Sunday secret for a productive and peaceful week—implementing a weekly habit of rest. The second secret, routine, is also essential. If we are intentional to have a routine—and prepare each week to successfully carry it out—life will become much more manageable and enjoyable. For me, Sundays provide the perfect time to do this. I can grab my planner, look over my weekly routine, and then sketch out my plan of attack. As a wise mentor once mentioned, "To find success, first plan your work and then work your plan."

Routines are important because they help us avoid decision fatigue. From the moment your feet hit the floor in the morning you are faced with a barrage of decisions. What will you wear today? What will you make for breakfast? When will you get things done around the house? When will you shop for groceries or fill up on gas? How will you remember to water the plants on the back patio, so they don't die? (You know, since you are already on purple petunia hanging basket number three, as they have croaked for lack of attention and H_2O!)

Routines can be imperative to good mental health. Knowing that our basic tasks of life are consistently covered helps us to worry less about making sure everything gets done. A routine can carry us through times of uncertainty, allowing us to run on autopilot instead of causing us stress as we try to remember all the tasks we must get done. Dr. Brad Brenner, PhD, of Therapy Group of NYC states, "By establishing a daily routine, we can set aside time to take care of tasks and focus on our mental and physical health. Routines are essential at every stage of life—from childhood and adolescence to adulthood. They help us cope with change, create healthy habits, improve interpersonal relationships, and reduce stress."[1]

For followers of Jesus, imperative to our plans coming to fruition is committing our schedules and obligations to the Lord. Psalm 143:8 is a fabulous anchor for us in this endeavor: "Let me experience your faithful love in the morning, for I trust in you. Reveal to me the way I should go because I appeal to you" (csb). Success in accomplishing our assignments each week doesn't hinge upon our diligence, creative planning, or any trick of the organizational trade. The key to realizing our goals is to make sure they are in line with what God would have us do. We must trust in him to give us the strength, energy, and wherewithal to work hard. We must pray to him to reveal to us the way we should go, believing confidently that he will answer us when we petition him (1 John 5:14).

> **If we are intentional to have a routine— and prepare each week to successfully carry it out—life will become much more manageable and enjoyable.**

So let's create a routine tailored for you in accordance with God's plans. Please know I am not referring to a strict schedule to carry out chores and complete duties within a specific time frame. Instead, my goal is this: to have a flexible routine that allows for interruptions from God and ministry to others. A schedule tethers tasks to a time frame. A routine lists your tasks in a particular order but accomplishes them as time allows. My weekly routine includes the obligations, activities, and tasks listed below. (Remember, this is just to provide you an example. You will come up with one specific to you in today's journaling section.)

- Administrative time to tackle paperwork, emails, etc.
- Creative time to write manuscripts, monthly columns, content for my newsletter, or social media posts.
- Home chores such as meal prep, laundry, cleaning, watering the plants, tending to the perennial and herb gardens, and menu planning and grocery shopping.
- Any appointments I have such as medical, church or committee meetings, podcast interviews or community involvement, etc.

On Sunday evening—when my early-riser husband goes to bed at least an hour before I do—I sit down with a steaming cup of peppermint tea, my planner (I use both paper and digital), and the above list chronicling my routine. I first put in any work or personal appointments. Then I look at the remaining white space while perusing the tasks I have for work. I write down each task in the free space where it will most suitably fit. When will I have a stretch of at least three hours of uninterrupted time to work on writing? When will I have maybe just forty-five minutes to answer emails? I write these tasks down.

Next, I turn my attention to chores at home, looking for a place for them to land. Some tasks are almost always on the same day and time slot. I water my indoor plants Wednesday evenings and Sunday mornings. (I think of it as "Water Wednesdays" and "Soaker Sundays.") During the warm months, I weed and water my herb and perennial gardens—along with my many potted plants and hanging baskets—early in the morning before beginning any work. For other tasks, I look for the time slot that will best work this week. It might be different from last week. For example, if I have a busy day at home on Tuesday with lots of radio and podcast interviews, it might make for a perfect day to do laundry and some meal prep for the days ahead. I can toss things into the washer and transfer them to the dryer between recordings, or chop some veggies and brown meat for meals during breaks. As for menu planning, grocery shopping, and the dreaded task of unloading and putting away all the groceries, I know I will need at least a two-hour slot of uninterrupted time for that. This week, that might be on Thursday.

Are you ready? Work through the questions below to craft your own personal routine. The results will bring you both productivity and peace of mind.

- First, commit your plans to the Lord. Read the following verses and then record what you learn about planning. What is your part, and what part does God play?

    Proverbs 16:3

    Proverbs 16:9

    Proverbs 19:21

    Proverbs 21:5

Ecclesiastes 3:1

Job 42:2

Matthew 6:33–34

Philippians 4:6

My part:

God's part:

- Using the space below, list out all the components of your weekly routine. Think about tasks at work, chores at home, responsibilities outside the home, etc. Generate a list you can use each week as you look over your planner and assign a targeted time slot to complete these obligations.

    Work:

Home:

Community and church:

Miscellaneous:

- Of the above items you chronicled, are there any that can be done repeatedly on the same day of the week, maybe even in the same time slot? (For example, laundry, grocery shopping, cleaning, etc.) List any that fall into that category below.

- Take a shot at sketching out your next week, placing tasks on your digital or paper planner. First, put time-specific appointments or commitments on the calendar. Then turn your attention to work. During what hours will you perform the tasks that relate to your job? For some, this may be something that is in a set time frame. Others may have flexibility to plan work tasks in the time slots best for you. Next, fill in household chores. Finally, see what space you have left and plan some leisure activities. During this exercise, try to leave one entire day open that will serve as your Sabbath.

- Now it is time to strategize your next Sabbath day! Choose your day. On that day, block off some time for planning your weekly routine. Also reserve time for doing something pleasurable that relaxes and refreshes you. If you can, also carve out a chunk of the day when you will physically rest or even get some shut-eye!

Doesn't it feel great to have your routine planned out? In the space below, pour out your heart to the Lord about designing and implementing a flexible routine. Ask him to help you to establish this weekly practice to bring you both a productive and a peaceful week.

• My Prayer •

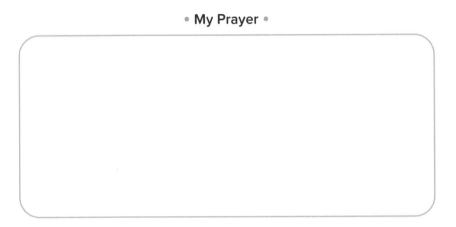

• Dig Deeper •

Listen to the *Don't Mom Alone* podcast with Heather MacFadyen, episode 300: "Healthy Habit Building" with Kat Lee.

• Highlighted Verse •

Let me experience
your faithful love in the morning,
for I trust in you.
Reveal to me the way I should go
because I appeal to you.

Psalm 143:8 CSB

Success in accomplishing our assignments each week doesn't hinge upon our diligence, creative planning, or any trick of the organizational trade.

The key to realizing our goals is to make sure they are **in line** with what God would have us do.

We must **trust in him** to give us the strength, energy, and wherewithal to work hard.

We must **pray to him** to reveal to us the way we should go.

day 18

The Real Reason You Just Can't Seem to Get Ahead

RUTH

I felt like I was running on a treadmill. Our kids' basketball and volleyball schedules felt like a full-time job! There was the house. My job. And my husband's health scare. I was using a lot of energy and getting things done. The problem was that I felt like I was not making any progress.

Have you ever felt like that?

Sometimes there are seasons or circumstances we can't help. There is just too much to be done. There is sickness. The unexpected. And even the tragic. We may not be in a position to keep up, let alone get ahead, because of life.

But there are other times, when the problem is not the work to be done or the amount of time we have. The issue is not a crowded schedule. It's not endless activities with our family. So what is it? It is YOU! Or ME! The problem is US! And what I mean by that is this: the real reason we can't get ahead sometimes is because we are utterly unorganized.

This is not an easy thing to admit. Because after all, we like to appear as though we have it together—as though we know what we are doing! But this is where we need to be honest. Most important, we need to be honest with ourselves about who we are. Or how we are doing.

As with anything that is wrong, there are usually warning signs. You know, those bright red or orange lights that are on the dashboard of our car? We might see one that is telling us we need to check the engine. Or the ones that signal low tire pressure. Maybe the oil light comes on telling us we need to change it.

The signs of disorganization may not be as easy to spot, but there are still ways we can figure out when we need to make changes. I see it on my desk first. It looks like a bomb went off! There are papers and sticky pads with reminders, phone numbers, and fragmented notes.

Sometimes we see it in our house or vehicles or piles of laundry. Phone calls don't get returned. Or perhaps we fail to respond to text messages.

Or we keep putting things off. We know there are things to do and decisions to be made, but we push them off until tomorrow. We get lazy. Procrastinate. All of these signals are screaming at us that there is a problem. The problem is not that we need more time—the problem is we are not using the time we have very well.

One of the keys to getting more done is not having more time, but using the time you do have in a wiser way.

The messes in our lives have a message—YOU are disorganized!

Proverbs 13:16 speaks to the importance of being thoughtful and organized: "All who are prudent act with knowledge, but fools expose their folly." To be prudent or wise is to be skilled. So the writer is saying there is a wise way to live and a foolish way to live. You can either walk through life with skill or just wing it! But eventually, winging it will no longer work.

The wise person acts with "knowledge, but fools expose their folly." Eventually the treadmill exposes them, and it becomes obvious that there is a need to grow in learning to plan, be thoughtful, and organized to succeed.

Being organized requires that we think ahead. It means we must consider the tasks and commitments in a coming week or month, then plan for them. It means we are thoughtful and we take time to create both a schedule and a strategy for how we are going to accomplish what needs to be done. We act with knowledge.

We all have the same amount of time in a day and week and month. The question is, how do we use that time? Do we budget our time in a similar way that we budget our money? If we don't, we end up wasting time instead of making the most of it.

Today, let's focus on taking back our time. One of the keys to getting more done is not having more time, but using the time you do have in a wiser way. How can you become more productive? Take a few moments to work your way through the following prompts and questions.

Taking Back Your Time

- I am most productive when I . . .

- I am most vulnerable to mismanaging time when I . . .

- What is one simple way you can begin to be more organized?

- Who in your life has the tendency to impact in a negative way how you use your time?

A passage that helps us with this endeavor is Ephesians 5:15–16. The apostle Paul is speaking about walking in faithfulness to God's will and being careful about how we live. The wise are those who make the most of every opportunity, being filled with the Holy Spirit, and giving thanks to God in all things. Take some time and read these verses several times. Once you have done this, reflect on the following questions:

- What does it mean to watch carefully how you live your life?

- How could you make "the most of every opportunity"?

- In what ways can the use of our time bring glory to God?

- Read Proverbs 13:16 again and complete the sentence below.
    I feel like God is asking me to live with greater wisdom and knowledge in the area of _____.

Take the next few moments to write out a prayer. Ask God to give you wisdom for how to use your time more effectively. Pray for the Holy Spirit's discernment in the area of relationships, commitments, and the use of your time.

• My Prayer •

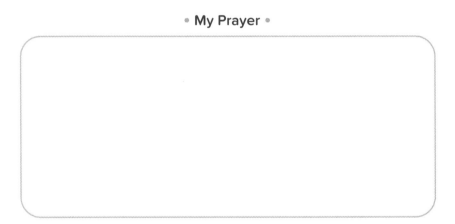

• Dig Deeper •

Listen to the *Get Your Hopes Up* podcast with Christy Wright, "5 Steps to Build a Good Morning Routine."
    Listen to the *Get Your Hopes Up* podcast with Christy Wright, "10 Ways to Maximize Your Time."

• Highlighted Verse •

All who are prudent act with knowledge, but fools expose their folly.

Proverbs 13:16

How to Ask for Help
When Life Goes Wrong

RUTH

When has life felt like too much to handle on your own? Along with my husband, who is a pastor, I have spent two and a half decades in ministry. Loving and serving others has been our life. We have loved ministry. For the most part, we have been the ones helping and carrying others.

All that changed when we got that dreaded phone call. It was an oncology nurse, the unfortunate one who had to call and communicate crushing news about my husband's blood work. He had cancer.

Like you, I have experienced different seasons and circumstances that left me unable to move on alone. My multiple miscarriages, then my husband's cancer diagnosis in 2018. Maybe you are in the middle of your own chaos right now—and life for you has gone terribly wrong.

When life gets hard, we can go from being the one carrying others to the one being carried.

This is never easy, for a lot of reasons. Asking others for help does not come naturally to me. I'd much rather be the strong one—the one who is doing the serving and giving and helping.

I often think of the story in Mark's gospel—the one where there are so many people crowding around Jesus while he is teaching in a home that a group of friends have to lower their paralyzed friend through the roof to get him to Jesus. What a picture of how we come to Jesus, not in our own strength, but by the grace of God.

Life for this man had gone terribly wrong. He can't help himself. What does he do? We're not sure of all the details, but we know he is literally carried by four of his friends. And so, the only hope he has is to be carried to the feet of Jesus. Mark writes,

Some men came, bringing to him a paralyzed man, carried by four of them. Since they could not get him to Jesus because of the crowd, they made an opening in the roof above Jesus by digging through it and then lowered the mat the man was lying on. When Jesus saw their faith, he said to the paralyzed man, "Son, your sins are forgiven."

Mark 2:3–5

There is a lot that could be said about this story, but what I want to highlight is the truth that we all find ourselves needing to be carried by others at some point. When life goes wrong—and it will if it hasn't already—don't be afraid or ashamed to ask for help.

> When life gets hard, we can go from being the one carrying others to the one being carried.

Allowing ourselves to be loved and served by others takes humility. It requires acknowledging that we don't have the wisdom or strength or resources to get through whatever we are facing. But our friends or family very well may. And it is okay to ask. It is okay to let them pick you up and carry you, to sustain you with their faith when yours may be weak.

The truth is, this is God's design for relationships—that we live *dependent* and not *independent* lives. We were made for community and deep meaningful friendship. At no time is this clearer than when life hits hard.

But it is also important to remember that we need to be grateful for how our friends *are able to* help us instead of focusing on how we *want* them to help us. God has wired or gifted each of us differently. Our friends or family members may very well be walking through their own challenges. So our different friends will love us differently, in whatever ways they can—but maybe not in a way we always want or wish them to. We need to humbly accept and be grateful for their help! God knows our needs and he knows exactly who we need at that time or season.

Today, let's take some time to discover where we need help most. Are there particular areas that have you overwhelmed and in need of someone's help?

Asking for Help

- What has you most discouraged or overwhelmed right now?

- Write down one to three areas you can't handle on your own right now and identify someone you may need to reach out to for help. Rarely is it the same person for all the situations we are facing in life. For example, you may need to reach out to someone different about a relationship than you will for financial help.

  - I need help with _____ so I am going to reach out to _____.

  - I need help with _____ so I am going to reach out to _____.

  - I need help with _____ so I am going to reach out to _____.

- Prayerfully consider why you find it difficult to ask for help. Ask God to give you the grace and humility to let others in.

- If you are not in a season when you need help, is there someone you know who is? Could you reach out and offer to help?

Two key passages for today are Genesis 2:18 and Mark 2:3–5. Read these passages and then reflect on the following questions:

- What is significant to you about God's statement in Genesis 2:18 that it is not good for us to be alone?

- In what ways were Adam and Eve meant to be good for one another? How should this look in a healthy and reciprocal friendship?

- In Mark 2:3–5, the man in need can do nothing but allow his friends to carry him. If you can imagine yourself in his place, what would be most challenging for you? For example, what would you struggle with as you allowed yourself to be the one carried?

- In what ways might Jesus be calling you to help carry someone else?

Take the next few moments to write out a prayer. Ask God to give you humility and the courage to ask for help when you need it.

• My Prayer •

• Dig Deeper •

Read *Find Your People: Building Deep Community in a Lonely World* by Jennie Allen.

• Highlighted Verse •

The Lord God said, "It is not good for the man to be alone. I will make a helper suitable for him."

Genesis 2:18

day 20

One Simple Trick to Reset Your Brain and Regain Your Joy

KAREN

A few summers ago, I found my soul in a very depleted state. We'd recently moved to a new town to be closer to my children's four grandparents. Then, very unexpectedly, they each passed away in less than three years, beginning just one month after we moved. I was also feeling stressed due to overcommitment in my church and community activities. A little while later, I felt my heart ricocheting all over as our first grandchild was born (extreme joy!), but then moved several states away with his parents when he was just five months old (severe sorrow). The combined weight of all the change, grief, loss, and pressure from too many activities was almost too much for me to bear.

It was during this time that I rummaged around, trying to find a helpful podcast. I listened to several during that summer right after the first grandparent passed away. However, just one tip from one podcast proved to be life-changing for me. (And I so wish I could remember which one, to give proper credit, but unfortunately, I've gone back and tried to figure it out—and simply can't!) This tip was a daily practice of spending seventeen minutes in silence, doing absolutely nothing.

The act of doing or thinking of nothing does not come easily to me. At any given point, I'm mulling over half a dozen things. I might be watching the news, but I am thinking about the chicken that I need to thaw out for supper, which reminds me that I still have dirty dishes on the counter, which reminds me that I'm out of dish soap and need to go to the grocery store, which reminds me that when I go to the grocery store, I also need to swing by the dry cleaners, which reminds me that the post office is next to the dry cleaners, and I am almost out of stamps. To be able to think nothing almost seems impossible to me. In fact, sometimes when my husband is sitting in his

112

favorite chair in the living room, staring out a window, I will ask him, "What'cha thinking?" and he will reply, "Nothing." I don't know how many hundreds of times I've said to him over the years, "Just *how* exactly do you do that? I want to know how to think nothing!"

However, after hearing the suggestion to practice a stretch of silence each day, I decided I would give it a try. That summer, each afternoon when my work-from-home work was done and before I tackled making dinner, I would wander out to the back of our property and plop myself in a lawn chair by the fire pit, nestled in a clump of beautiful woods. Squirrels chased each other up and down trees, birds sang in the treetops, and I tried my best to just look up at the fluffy clouds in the sky playing hide and seek among the leaves and think absolutely nothing.

> **Somehow, being silent and thinking nothing— while doing nothing— for seventeen minutes each day seems to hit the restart button on the mind and ease my frenzied soul.**

At first, this was exceedingly difficult. So many thoughts popped into my brain. I learned to take a small notebook and pen with me to jot down anything that came to mind that I needed to take care of later. This helped me to focus more on quieting my thoughts and centering my soul. I tried to simply observe what was going on around me or just listen to the sounds of the neighborhood—dogs barking, children playing, the ice cream truck turning the corner and heading down our street. If I did feel my mind start to fret, I would simply repeat a short prayer: "Jesus, quiet my mind and settle my soul."

As the seasons rolled on, I learned to do this when the autumn leaves were falling or inside during the cold months, cuddled up under a woven cotton throw blanket, staring at the flickering flames of my fireplace. Somehow, being silent and thinking nothing—while *doing* nothing—for seventeen minutes each day seems to hit the restart button on the mind and ease my frenzied soul.

So often, as followers of Jesus, we think about all the things we should be *doing* for the Lord. But I happened upon a verse over a decade ago that instead paints a lovely and soothing picture for us of quiet moments spent just *being* before the Lord. It is found in the book of Zephaniah, a prophetic book written during the reign of King Josiah, most likely between 635 and 625 BC. This book carries a message of God's sovereignty over all the nations and his righteous judgment that is to come. However, it also stresses how God will bless those who repent and trust in him. I find it fascinating that in the middle of a book about sin and judgment, we read this:

> The Lord your God in your midst, The Mighty One, will save; He will rejoice over you with gladness, He will quiet *you* with His love, He will rejoice over you with singing.
>
> Zephaniah 3:17 NKJV

Our English phrase "He will quiet" in this verse is translated from a singular Hebrew word, *charash* (pronounced *khaw-rash'*), which means to cut in, to construct, to engrave, to perfect. I love the picture this paints! Sometimes I need the Lord to cut into my day—as only he can—engraving his love upon my heart and perfecting me to be more like his Son. I desperately need him to quiet me, and this often happens as I think of him rejoicing over me with singing and gladness.

Will you take on the challenge of spending seventeen minutes a day in silence, attempting to say, think, and do nothing? The following questions and suggestions will help you in this endeavor.

- Have you ever tried just sitting in silence? If so, what did you experience? If not, why do you think you have never attempted it before?

- Being silent not only has spiritual benefits, but there are physical and emotional ones as well. An article by the Cleveland Clinic asserts, "We can use calm, quiet moments to tap into a different part of the nervous system that helps shut down our bodies' physical response to stress."[1] The article goes on to say that "being still and silent" can help lower blood pressure, decrease heart rate, steady breathing, and reduce muscle tension, as well as increase focus and cognition.[2] Which of these physical changes could you benefit from?

- Look over your calendar for the next few days. Try to block off seventeen minutes each day when you will try this exercise. You might need to get up a little earlier or delay bedtime a bit to fit it in.

When the time comes for your first session of silence, keep in mind the following:

- Make sure you find a space where you will be comfortable and free from interruptions.
- Leave your phone behind but take a notepad and paper so you can jot down anything that does pop into your mind that you will need to do later but are afraid you might forget.
- Try your very best to just be an observer, looking around and taking in the sights. Listen also for the sounds you hear. Feel the wind on your face if you are outside or smell the scent of a candle burning indoors during winter. Think about your five senses and experiencing the moment rather than allowing your brain to mull over thoughts.
- Have a short prayer in your mind that you can repeat out loud if thoughts start to invade your mind and distract you. Some examples are, "Jesus, clear my mind and settle my soul," or "Father, help me focus on the moment and not fret."
- If you feel that you simply must think something, picture the Lord—as in the days of Zephaniah—rejoicing over you with gladness and singing and quieting you with his love.
- End your seventeen minutes thanking God in prayer for the calm and quiet and for loving you with an everlasting love.

In the space below, write out a prayer to God about your desire to start spending an uninterrupted silent time each day to help reset your soul.

• My Prayer •

• Dig Deeper •

Listen to the *John Mark Comer Teachings* podcast, "The Power of Quiet in a World of Noise | Unhurrying with a Rule of Life E4."

• Highlighted Verse •

The Lord your God in your midst,
The Mighty One, will save;
He will rejoice over you with gladness,
He will quiet you with His love,
He will rejoice over you with singing.

Zephaniah 3:17 NKJV

Pursuing the Passions God Has for Me

Priorities determined? Perspective in place? Great! Now it is time to pursue the passions God has for you. We are halfway through our journey! Days 21 through 30 will help you further explore your passions, giftings, and natural talents with an eternal perspective and in relation to your people and your projects. You will learn strategies for how to stick to your goals as well as how to avoid being paralyzed by perfectionism or having your productivity derailed by procrastination. Most of all, you will learn to prioritize times of rest to help you refuel and be ready to work again, with excellence and to the glory of God. So grab your pen and your Bible, as you continue to learn how to prioritize your passions, create habits of productivity, and refuel with times of rest.

Chasing Your What

RUTH

"What am I supposed to do with my life?" I remember thinking. Now, years removed from the first time I asked myself that question, I can see that the question originally started with more of a yearning—an ache. I remember I wanted to do something—anything—to make my life count! I don't remember exactly how old I was when I first started asking the question. But it was one that I would ask and wrestle with over and over again in the years to come.

I tried to answer the question in various ways in the many years that followed. I want to be a wife and mom. I want to start a blog. Maybe I was supposed to be a speaker. Or perhaps I should start a business. Singing had been a huge part of my life since I was a little girl, so maybe I was supposed to be a worship leader. There were all sorts of things I thought I should do or could do. I was consumed with searching for and finding my calling.

Haven't we all experienced that? Maybe in different ways and at different times. We've probably all wrestled with our calling or vocation. And at the heart of that desire to live out our calling is the desire to make our life count. To do something that matters!

Not too long ago, I came across a quote from St. Therese of Lisieux, a follower of Jesus who lived in France toward the end of the nineteenth century. She was a woman who suffered greatly in a variety of ways, and her life was cut short as a result; she died at the age of twenty-four. While there is much we can learn from her life, one of the things she is most famous for saying that stuck out to me is "At last I have found my vocation; *it is love!*"[1]

We spend so much time and energy searching for our calling, yet what St. Therese discovered was what we also know all too well—that what

Jesus taught was the greatest commandment. Our first calling, or first vocation, is to love.

In Matthew 22:35–39, when one of the religious leaders asked Jesus what the greatest commandment in the Law was, "Jesus replied: 'Love the Lord your God with all your heart and with all your soul and with all your mind.' This is the first and greatest commandment. And the second is like it: 'Love your neighbor as yourself.' All the Law and the Prophets hang on these two commandments" (Matthew 22:37–40).

Our first calling, or first vocation, is to love.

Everything hangs on love. We see this theme repeated over and over again throughout the New Testament. We are to know the depth of God's love for us and then live a life of love in response!

I had spent so many years chasing after what I was supposed to do. And as obvious as it may seem, I was missing our calling. Not mine. Or yours. But all of ours, as followers of Jesus. While we may all follow Jesus differently, we all share this first and primary vocation to love God and love others. We are to "be Love," no matter what we do!

So whatever job we have, whatever the role we may fill or the title we possess, our greatest calling is to be Love!

Today, we are going to focus on finding greater freedom to love the way Jesus wants us to love. True freedom begins inside of us. We can't love deeply and freely if certain sins have us enslaved. So our goal is to prayerfully identify various barriers that are preventing us from loving God and loving others as we should.

Below, write down any barriers that come to mind that you believe are keeping you from being Love. For example, is insecurity a barrier for you? Is there an unhealthy or unholy ambition for success you have noticed in your own heart? What about the need to have people's approval? Or maybe it is the need to be loved by others that is preventing you from loving others like Christ.

Barriers to Freedom

1. _____

2. _____

3. _____

4. _____

5. _____

Now that you have identified specific barriers, identify a key verse or passage of Scripture that will help you overcome that barrier. You may use a concordance in the back of your Bible or an online resource such as biblegateway.com. For example, if you identified people pleasing as a barrier, you might write out the words to Galatians 1:10, which says, "Am I now trying to win the approval of human beings, or of God? Or am I trying to please people? If I were still trying to please people, I would not be a servant of Christ." Now write the barrier and corresponding verse below. For example, people pleasing: Galatians 1:10.

1.

2.

3.

4.

5.

Next, let's identify specific people in your life Jesus is calling you to love. This might be a difficult neighbor, a cantankerous family member, a new co-worker, or a discouraged friend. Think about all the places you spend time each week, especially the workplace. There are bound to be souls God is nudging you to love.

Once you have identified the person, next to their name, write out whether Jesus is calling you to love them more deeply or more freely. To love someone deeply might mean loving more sacrificially and being more patient—blessing with no expectations. To love someone freely might mean letting someone go, not holding on to a friendship in the same way you did before, practicing forgiveness, etc.

1.

2.

3.

4.

5.

6.

Finally, take the next few moments to write out a prayer. Ask God to cultivate the love of Jesus in you through the power of his Spirit. Include in that prayer specific people Jesus is asking you to love in more significant ways.

• My Prayer •

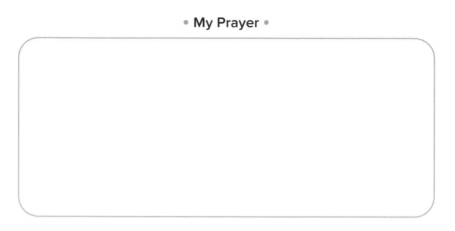

• Dig Deeper •

Read *The Story of a Soul: The Autobiography of St. Therese of Lisieux.*

• Highlighted Verse •

Am I now trying to win the approval of human beings, or of God? Or am I trying to please people? If I were still trying to please people, I would not be a servant of Christ.

Galatians 1:10

day 22

How to Set
Life Goals That Stick

RUTH

Our family has always loved setting goals. Each year, as January rolls around, we typically buy new journals for everyone. We take time toward the end of December to think and pray about the coming year. We then map out in our new journals those goals we believe God is calling us to pursue.

While we've done this fairly consistently as our kids have gotten older, one thing we haven't always done consistently is actually stick to our goals! They look and sound great on paper. The problem is that by March, we've either forgotten or given up!

Sound familiar? Setting life goals that stick is hard. So what do we do? Or what *should* we do?

Ambition is not enough. Hard work won't cut it. Even being driven won't always guarantee a goal will stick. So, as followers of Jesus, how do we set life goals that we actually keep pursuing? The answer is we need to set goals that are rooted in our *calling*.

A calling is greater than something you want to achieve. It's bigger and more important than a bucket list or goal. A calling originates not with you, but with God. It is something you believe and have discerned that God is asking you to do—and has wired you to do. (Remember, as we mentioned in the last entry, our first calling, or first vocation, is to love.)

We are all called by God's grace to turn from our sins and turn to Jesus as Savior. This is what many have termed a *universal call*. It is universal because, as 1 Timothy 2:4–6 says, God "wants all people to be saved and to come to a knowledge of the truth. For there is one God and one mediator between God and mankind, the man Christ Jesus, who gave himself as a ransom for all people."

But while we are all called to follow Jesus, we are also all called to follow Jesus *differently*. This is what we mean when describing our *unique calling*. It is specific to YOU!

This unique calling is based on your gifts and abilities. It is informed and fueled by your life experiences. And while God's calling might feel mysterious at times, it is the way Jesus is inviting you to love him and love others. It is how he wants to live his life through you.

A calling originates not with you, but with God.

Sometimes this calling is obvious and discovered quite easily. Other times, it is discerned slowly and with the help of others. We can determine, with God's help, our unique calling through life's experiences, our successes, failures, and even our suffering.

For some, this calling might be to become a teacher. For others, to work in a factory or build a family. Pursue full-time ministry in a church or nonprofit organization. Give ourselves to writing. Work with finances. The list goes on!

We see this example in the life of the apostle Paul at the beginning of his first letter to the church in Corinth. He writes, "Paul, called to be an apostle of Christ Jesus by the will of God, and our brother Sosthenes, To the church of God in Corinth, to those sanctified in Christ Jesus and called to be his holy people, together with all those everywhere who call on the name of our Lord Jesus Christ—their Lord and ours" (1 Corinthians 1:1–2).

Paul understood his life was not his own. The point of his life was to point others to Jesus. He had been "called to be an apostle of Christ Jesus" not because it was his dream, but because it was the "will of God."

So how do you set life goals that stick? It begins with knowing your calling, which will sustain you when life gets hard and you are tempted to give up on your work or those goals you set.

Today, begin by assessing your calling. Then begin to set goals—goals that are rooted in your calling. Let's take a closer look at what you believe God has wired you to do. And then let's examine whether your goals line up with your calling.

A Closer Look at Your Calling

- What goals have you set that didn't stick and why?

- How would you describe the difference between a dream and a calling?

- Which goals do you have that are not rooted in your calling?

- What are some specific and practical ways to make sure you stick to the goals you have set?

A relevant passage on this subject is 1 Corinthians 1:1–2. As the apostle Paul is beginning his letter to the church in Corinth, he describes his calling. Prayerfully read and then reread these verses. Once you have done this, reflect on the following questions:

- How does Paul describe his calling?

- Read 2 Corinthians 4:7–9. What enabled Paul to endure various hardships?

- Why is understanding calling so important for what we choose to pursue?

- What specific hardships is God encouraging you to persevere through in this season?

Take the next few moments to write out a prayer. Ask God to give you clarity on your calling. If you are struggling, ask him for help to endure. And seek his wisdom on what it is he wants you to pursue—goals that will actually stick.

• My Prayer •

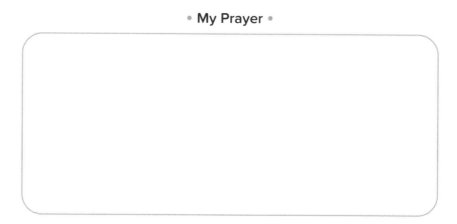

• Dig Deeper •

Read *Courage and Calling: Embracing Your God-Given Potential* by Gordon T. Smith.

• Highlighted Verses •

Paul, called to be an apostle of Christ Jesus by the will of God, and our brother Sosthenes, To the church of God in Corinth, to those sanctified in Christ Jesus and called to be his holy people, together with all those everywhere who call on the name of our Lord Jesus Christ—their Lord and ours.

1 Corinthians 1:1–2

day 23

How to Stop Being Paralyzed by Perfectionism

KAREN

"Your job is to sit by the front door in a chair, sipping a soda, and pointing which way each person should go." These were the words of a dear friend who was among the dozen or so people helping us to move into our new home that day. She could sense I was wound up, tuckered out, and awfully anxious. I just wanted every item to be carefully unpacked and perfectly placed in our new home—items I'd spent weeks meticulously packing in boxes. Knowing she was being wise, I eventually took her advice, sat down, and commenced pointing. However, behind my forced smile, my mind was spinning, trying to think through just where everything should go.

Our family of five had just moved out of our tiny starter home that was barely 900 square feet. This new house wasn't huge by any measure, but it was a little over 1,100 feet square with a finished basement where we would have a living room and our homeschool room/office. The whole family was excited, including me. But I also let my perfectionism kick into high gear, desiring that everything look tidy and fit just so.

There are many reasons we struggle with perfectionism. There are also varying degrees of it. Some people tend to be meticulous in every area of life. Others are perfectionistic only about one or two aspects of life, such as the look of their home, their performance at work, or the behavior of someone in their family. For me, perfectionism started early. A competitive personality, coupled with some anxiousness I felt due to being the child of a broken home and all wrapped up in a constant desire for attention, made me chase hard after perfection. Whether it was getting the highest grade on the chemistry test or winning the head captain position at cheerleading tryouts, I wanted to achieve excellence so that my life looked—and felt—perfect. This tendency only grew worse as I became an adult and now had a dwelling to tend to.

Now, some might think pursuing perfection is a worthy endeavor. After all, we're just trying to be conscientious and careful, right? But pursuing perfection sets us up for falling short of our lofty goals. And when we don't meet our objective, we experience feelings of failure. The desire to avoid such feelings leads to an unfortunate condition: we become paralyzed perfectionists, unable to even *begin* a project because we are stuck in a cycle of overthinking how best to make it turn out flawless.

My experience with this—as well as being both the wife and the mother of humans who have the same tendency—has propelled me to acquire some strategies for preventing perfectionistic tendencies from paralyzing me. I needed to learn how to free myself whenever I feel the fastidiousness creeping into my behavior, causing me to feel stuck.

> **We can trust the Lord to help us remember the truth: He is perfect, and we are not. He will meet us in our weaknesses, making us more like Jesus in the process.**

Primary in helping me to overcome analysis paralysis was a little peek into a conversation in the New Testament between Jesus and the apostle Paul. At the opening of 2 Corinthians 12, Paul mentions a thorn in his flesh, stating that it was sent by Satan to torment him. He tells the Corinthians that he pleaded with God on three different occasions for him to remove this thorn from his flesh. Biblical scholars have debated through the years just what this thorn was. Some think it was a combative person who was making life difficult for him. However, he specifically mentions that this thorn was in his physical flesh. So most theologians think it was a physical ailment, perhaps poor eyesight. Sometimes he had someone else write his letters, or he would mention that he was signing his own name in large letters, indicating, perhaps, that his ability to see was growing dim (see Galatians 6:11). What was the Lord's answer to Paul's triple request for relief from this thorn? In 2 Corinthians 12:9–10 CSB, Paul tells us, "But he said to me, 'My grace is sufficient for you, for my power is perfected in weakness.' Therefore, I will most gladly boast all the more about my weaknesses, so that Christ's power may reside in me. So I take pleasure in weaknesses, insults, hardships, persecutions, and in difficulties, for the sake of Christ. For when I am weak, then I am strong."

Having perfectionist tendencies that paralyze our productivity might not be as dire as a physical thorn in the flesh. Nevertheless, we can adopt an outlook from the response given by the Lord to Paul. If God's grace was enough for him, it can also be enough for us. If God's power is made perfect in weakness, we shouldn't shy away from our own weaknesses.

Instead, we can admit them to the Lord and petition his help during those times when an aspect of our personality is making us unproductive, inefficient, or incapable of moving forward. In fact, we can be like Paul and decide to delight in our weakness!

The Greek word translated as "most gladly" here is *hédista* (pronounced *hay'-dis-tah*), which also means most pleasantly, sweetly, and without regret or reservation. What an attitude shift from how we normally feel when we are battling perfectionism! We can trust the Lord to help us remember the truth: He is perfect, and we are not. He will meet us in our weaknesses, making us more like Jesus in the process.

Here are a few perspective-shifting statements for you to preach to yourself when battling perfectionism. Put a star next to the one that most speaks to you, then answer the question that follows the four statements.

- Something is better than nothing. Therefore, I will take action and at least commence, knowing it won't be perfect, but it will be a start.

- No one gets it right on the first draft. Therefore, I will do the work of getting off the blank page, remembering that there will be many tweaks and revisions before the project is through.

- Perfectionism is not my friend—in fact, it can be my archenemy. When I feel critical thoughts rising up, making me feel paralyzed, I will fight against them and seek to work steadily and cheerfully, knowing that the finished product will take some time and I need to be patient.

- Perfectionism can steal my joy. However, I will not let this be the case. Instead, I will, like Paul, rejoice in this weakness and delight in all the Lord is teaching me, remembering that in my weakness, he is strong.

Now think of a situation in which you typically feel paralyzed by perfectionism. How can what you have learned today help you to behave differently in the future? Write out some steps you will take the next time you start to feel stuck and paralyzed by perfectionism.

Lastly, write out a heartfelt prayer to the Father, asking him to help you to not be derailed by perfectionism, but to cheerfully do your best work.

• My Prayer •

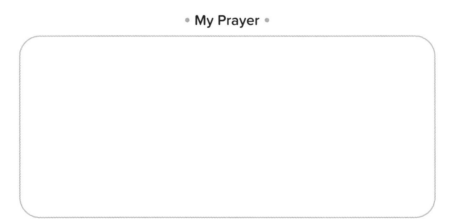

• Dig Deeper •

Watch *Beloved Women with Christina Patterson* YouTube video: "How to Overcome Perfectionism."

• Highlighted Verses •

But he said to me, "My grace is sufficient for you, for my power is per-fected in weakness." Therefore, I will most gladly boast all the more about my weaknesses, so that Christ's power may reside in me. So I take pleasure in weaknesses, insults, hardships, persecutions, and in difficulties, for the sake of Christ. For when I am weak, then I am strong.

2 Corinthians 12:9–10 CSB

When Quitting Is Winning

RUTH

Several years ago, my husband and I bought some new furniture. Not the kind that comes assembled and ready to put in place. That would be too easy! Nope, we bought the kind that comes in parts—lots of parts.

We were filled with excitement. And of course, visions of what our family room was going to look like with these new additions. Then the delivery truck came.

Our furniture arrived in boxes. Once we actually got the boxes open, we quickly discovered this was going to be a slow process. We found instructions the length of some books of the Bible. Small metal tools. Wooden pegs and lots of other pieces that needed to be set or glued in just the right spots. We were both overwhelmed. But only one of us was NOT willing to give up—that was ME!

I'll be the first to admit that I am not one to give in easily. I like to see a project of any kind through to completion. I have never been a quitter. So as much as I wanted to go to sleep that night, I refused to until we got it done!

Maybe you are like me and hate to give up or give in. On the other hand, perhaps you find it easy to know when to throw in the towel. The truth is, there are clearly times we need to press on. We all have faced seasons and circumstances that required persistence, hard work, and NOT quitting. Biblical examples and encouragement to endure are numerous (Matthew 10:22; Romans 2:7; Hebrews 12:1–2; James 1:2–4). But is quitting always bad? Are there times and situations in which quitting is actually a good thing? I think there are.

Sometimes Quitting Is Winning.

There is a verse in the Old Testament that gives us a clue to separating what we want at times from what God wants. This can also help us decide when quitting is okay. In Proverbs 19:21, we read that "Many are the plans in a person's heart, but it is the Lord's purpose that prevails" (emphasis added).

The writer is reminding us that there are plans we make. There are things we commit to. We might say there are dreams we have. But not all of this is always from God.

Not all our dreams are God's desires. And our plans don't always line up with God's purposes. Because of this, we need to be open and sensitive to how the Holy Spirit is leading us. We need to be honest. Teachable. Willing to accept when we are to keep persevering and when it is time to call it quits.

> **Not all our dreams are God's desires.**

Quitting might involve your job. A volunteer commitment. Maybe you are wrestling with a relationship with a friend. Or it could be a dream or set of priorities you have established for this season of your life.

Sometimes it becomes obvious that our plans are not God's purposes. And there are times when we need to recognize that a change in our circumstances might mean a change in a commitment we had made previously. Then there are those things we are involved in that are actually getting in the way of giving ourselves more fully to God's calling or priorities for us.

Whatever it is you are considering quitting, I am confident that as you prayerfully pursue God's will, he will make it clear. As with anything, I encourage you to pray. Search God's Word. Reach out to a trusted and godly leader, friend, or family member. And above all, know that God is in control. He has promised to guide and direct your steps (Proverbs 3:5–6).

Today, let's dig a little deeper into trying to discern when it is okay to quit. While this is not an exhaustive list, consider the following questions to help you decide when to persevere and when to bring things to a halt.

Questions to Help You Discern if Quitting is Winning:

- Is this taking me away from my calling or purpose?
- Is it causing me to compromise spiritually in any way?
- Am I at risk or danger in any way?
- Are there important relationships that are being sacrificed?
- Do I really have time for this in this season or set of circumstances?
- Is this bringing joy?
- Do I find myself loving God more because of this?
- Is God asking me to grow and learn through this experience rather than run from it?

An important Scripture on this topic is Proverbs 19:21. Reread this short verse. There are times when we quit for the wrong reasons. We lack strength or moral fortitude to keep pressing on. And then there are times when quitting is the right thing to do. We need faith and courage. The following questions are meant to continue to help you discern when quitting is winning.

- When do you remember quitting something too soon? What did that reveal about your character?

- Was there a time that persevering led to greater Christlikeness in your life? In what way?

- What moral qualities or character traits do you think are necessary to quit sometimes?

- What is Jesus asking you to persevere in and what is he asking you to quit?

Take the next few moments to write out a prayer. Ask God to give you wisdom and discernment. Seek his will for what you need to keep enduring as well as for those commitments, obligations, or relationships you may need to quit.

• My Prayer •

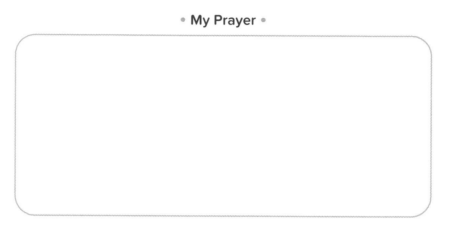

• Dig Deeper •

Watch *Proverbs 31 Ministries* YouTube video: "How to Focus on What's Important with Lara Casey."

• Highlighted Verse •

Many are the plans in a person's heart, but it is the Lord's purpose that prevails.

Proverbs 19:21

Sometimes it becomes
obvious that our plans
are **not God's purposes.**

And there are times when
we need to recognize
that a **change** in our
circumstances might mean
a change in a commitment
we had made previously.

Then there are those things
we are involved in that
are actually getting in the
way of giving ourselves
more fully to God's calling
or **priorities** for us.

day 25

When Life Feels Urgent

RUTH

Have you ever come to the end of a day and felt like you didn't accomplish anything? Or maybe you have felt that every day is like being on a fast-paced treadmill. You are just doing your best to keep putting one foot in front of the other!

Life can feel urgent. It is easy to go through a day, a week, or a month externally, feeling as though you are always responding or reacting to something. Or someone. But is this really the way to live? Is this really the life Jesus lived and the one he invites us into? The good news is that Jesus offers us a different way.

Just imagine for a minute what it must have been like for the eternal Son of God—Jesus, the second Person of the Trinity—to be constrained to a human body, to know the limitations of humanity.

It's what theologians call the *incarnation* or *enfleshment* of God. Jesus, who is God, was also human. He "became flesh and made his dwelling among us" (John 1:14). He is the "image of the invisible God" (Colossians 1:15). "God was pleased to have all his fullness dwell in him" (Colossians 1:19).

So Jesus loves your humanity. How do we know? Because he took it on. He knows what it is like to grow weary. To feel hungry. Get thirsty. Or come to the end of a day and need to rest. In his humanity, Jesus knows what it is like to have limitations.

While we often live with a sense of panic, Jesus always lived with purpose. Jesus was focused without being frenzied. He came to do his Father's will—but he did it within the boundaries or limitations of humanity. Flesh and blood. Why is this good news for us?

It frees us from feeling that we have to do everything. Or that we *can* do everything! It enables us to do "enough" each day. Jesus doesn't ask us to do the impossible. He knows we can't. He asks us to be faithful in the real-life circumstances of whatever season we are in. And just our desire to please him pleases him.

The God who knows our limitations, and even entered into them for our sake, is gentle with us. Patient. He understands we can't do it all. And we certainly can't do it in our own strength. It's all his grace.

> **While we often live with a sense of panic, Jesus always lived with purpose. Jesus was focused without being frenzied.**

He asks us for a life of humble trust and surrender. He asks us to be faithful. He takes whatever we can give him and then he does the rest. The real heavy lifting! After all, it is all his work anyway.

What he wants from us is not more. He wants us to be dependent. His heart for us is not urgency, but the confidence that he can take whatever we are able to give him today and use it for his purposes.

Today, as we focus on moving away from a life of frenzy or feelings of urgency, let's explore the difference between panic and purpose.

Panic or Purpose

- How would you describe your feeling of living with urgency each day?

- What causes you to feel panic or urgency most often?

- In what ways does this lead you toward independence from God instead of dependence on God?

- If you were to pull out of one activity or commitment, what would it be and why?

Two key verses on this topic are John 1:1 and 14. Take time to reread these verses. Focus on the mystery of Jesus' incarnation. Think about how this relates to your own limitations and the freedom of dependency Jesus wants to cultivate in your own life.

- What does it mean that Jesus loves and understands our humanity? How is this an encouragement to you?

- Read John 15:1–4 in the New King James Version of the Bible. How can you practically move from trying to accomplish more to abiding more?

- What example from Jesus' life shows him living with limitations?

And finally, what are one or two ways you can live more freely by living with limitations?

Take the next few moments to write out a prayer. Ask God to give you direction and insight into living within your limitations.

• **My Prayer** •

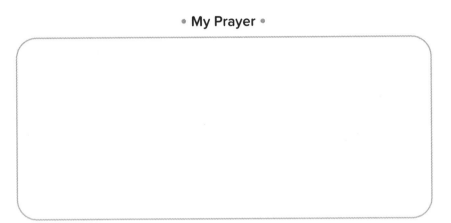

• **Dig Deeper** •

Read *Sacred Rest: Recover Your Life, Renew Your Energy, Restore Your Sanity* by Saundra Dalton-Smith, MD.

• **Highlighted Verse** •

The Word became flesh and made his dwelling among us. We have seen his glory, the glory of the one and only Son, who came from the Father, full of grace and truth.

John 1:14

day 26

How to Say No, Once and For All

KAREN

Has your mouth ever gotten you in a mighty mess, all because you uttered a simple *yes*? You were asked to take on a responsibility, to spearhead a project, or maybe do something simple like watching your friend's child or finding an online link for your sister-in-law. So many of us have a hard time saying no. It can cause us great grief—or maybe just slight inconvenience—all because we are afraid.

Have you ever thought of people pleasing in that way—that it means you are afraid? We'd like to think we say yes too much because we are being kind. However, as a person who has suffered from the disease to please most of my life, I can tell you that at the core of it is fear. We are afraid of disappointing someone, of upsetting someone, or of having someone not view us as capable, compassionate, or conscientious. So we just keep letting the yeses roll off our lips, helping or placating others. Our actions make them glad while making ourselves glum.

Giving in to this fear causes us to become known as a yes-man, or yes-woman. We become an easy target for someone who has created a crisis and now needs our help. They turn to us because they know we will say yes to their request. They've observed a pattern in us over the years that allows them to predict just what our response will be. Author Tony Gaskins summed up this process vividly when he said on the social media platform X, "You teach people how to treat you; by what you allow, what you stop, and what you reinforce."[1]

That was so eye-opening to me the first time I read it nearly a decade ago. I realized how I'd taught other people that they could ask for anything—from a small favor to a colossal request—and they could count on me to come through. With each ask, I felt a tug on my heart. And I was tempted to answer only in the way I knew the other person would want me to. This temptation was so strong that I fell for it time and time again until, after decades of giving in to people pleasing, I started to feel the effects physically. My stress level had risen to the point that I was having trouble sleeping, my left eye twitched uncontrollably several times a day, and I even started to suffer mild panic attacks. With all I had going on in my life at the time, I simply could not keep up my people-pleasing ways. I had to stop giving in to the temptation to say yes.

> **We are afraid of disappointing someone, of upsetting someone, or of having someone not view us as capable. So we keep letting the yeses roll off our lips, helping or placating others. Our actions make them glad while making ourselves glum.**

Thankfully, as always, God's Word holds the key to any predicament we face. I not only scoured Scripture for any verses that might help me stop giving in to this temptation, I actually memorized one! It was so empowering to have this verse pop up in my mind when I was tempted to give in and say yes. That verse is 1 Corinthians 10:13. "No temptation has come upon you except what is common to humanity. But God is faithful; he will not allow you to be tempted beyond what you are able, but with the temptation he will also provide the way out so that you may be able to bear it" (CSB).

The original Greek word for our English phrase "bear it" is *hupopheró* (pronounced *hoop-of-er'-o*), and it means "to bear by being under, to endure,"[2] or to be carried away safely from danger. When we decide to answer truthfully, we can endure the temptation, bearing up under it, and find sweet relief.

I will admit this is easier said than done. This verse is not just some magical incantation we can recite when we are being tempted to say yes. It is just the starting point. Two other tactics have come into play as I have learned to break free from the prison of people pleasing. The first is prayer.

I know that sounds so simplistic, but I make it a matter of prayer each morning. I ask the Lord to help me to not be so afraid of the opinions and reactions of others that I don't answer honestly. This has helped immensely in my journey to not be bound by the expectations of others. God cares about even what might seem to be insignificant in our day-to-day life and our relationships. I challenge you to also begin to pray a similar prayer each day.

The second strategy is to pre-decide what I will say when I'm asked to do something I know I don't have the capability or conviction to do. (Note: Of course, there are times when we do have the capacity and conviction to say yes, and we wholeheartedly should! The key is recognizing the difference.) Pre-deciding means that I arm myself with some language to use so I don't find myself fumbling for words and then ending up saying yes when I shouldn't. Here are a few examples:

- "I truly wish I could say yes to what you want me to do, but I simply don't have any leeway right now to add anything more to my schedule."
- "I realize you need help and I care about you. However, I wouldn't be able to give this project the focus and thoughtfulness it warrants, so I will be praying you find someone capable of doing just that."
- "Thank you so much for asking. I'm honored you thought of me. However, God has really been dealing with me lately about my inability to say no to people. It really is a struggle in my life. But I know you will still love me when I tell you that I'm just not able to add this to my schedule."
- "I really value our friendship, so I hesitate to say no. However, I know you will appreciate my being honest with you."
- "I wish I could say yes, but I have to pass. Please don't let that prevent you from asking me in the future. I care about you and what you have going on in life."

Arming yourself with such statements gives you the confidence to speak the truth. And speaking the truth is a gift to the person who is asking something of you. You don't want your relationship to be based on dishonesty. Additionally, you will not be falsely teaching them that you are someone incapable of saying no. Those people who are your true friends will still love you, even when you can't always say yes to their requests.

Now it is your turn. Read through the above examples again. Then, in the space below write out two or three of your own predetermined statements you can use when you feel tempted to say yes, but know you should say no.

Prayer is foundational to overcoming this temptation. Draft a prayer to God below asking him to help you to honestly and sweetly say no when you know you should. Also ask for discernment for those times that you should say yes to a request.

• My Prayer •

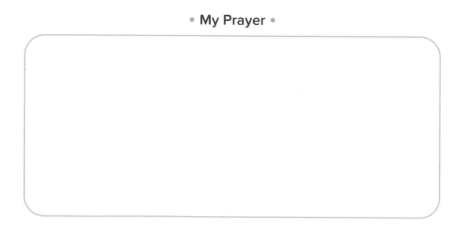

• Dig Deeper •

Read *When Making Others Happy Is Making You Miserable: How to Break the Pattern of People Pleasing and Confidently Live Your Life* by Karen Ehman.

• Highlighted Verse •

No temptation has come upon you except what is common to humanity. But God is faithful; he will not allow you to be tempted beyond what you are able, but with the temptation he will also provide the way out so that you may be able to bear it.

1 Corinthians 10:13 CSB

day 27

The One Thing You Can Do Today to Safeguard Your Rest

RUTH

Have you ever felt guilty for just taking a break? Or like you are going to get in trouble for not getting enough done today? Sometimes this pressure comes from others, but often we place this burden on ourselves! We love to go. And do. We are often thinking about what needs to be accomplished today. These concerns are real. And depending on the season of life you are in, these feelings of needing to get things done are legitimate.

So we can wrestle with our own thoughts. We try to quiet what we are thinking, while sometimes suppressing what our soul needs most.

There is so much on my plate today.
I need to get up and get going.
I'm too busy to pray. Too busy to read my Bible today.

But here is where we need to stop. And just pause, in order to remember a simple truth. Our greatest need is not to accomplish something, but to abide with Someone.

If we are to have anything to give to others, we must first receive it by getting alone with God. Jesus tells us to come to him. He reminds us that our greatest need is to find rest in him.

Come to me, all you who are weary and burdened, and I will give you rest. Take my yoke upon you and learn from me, for I am gentle and humble in heart, and you will find rest for your souls. For my yoke is easy and my burden is light.

Matthew 11:28–30

146

To the weary, go to Jesus.
To the burdened, go to Jesus.
To the worn out and overwhelmed, go to Jesus.

His promise is that he gives us rest. And then he tells us to take his yoke upon us. What is this yoke? It is his way of life. It is his teaching. We come to find rest in him, but then we learn to be like him.

He reassures us that he is "gentle and humble in heart" (v. 29). He is patient with us and compassionate toward us. Ever calling us forward and onward. But first, he calls us close. And teaches us to abide with him if we are to bear any fruit for his kingdom (John 15:1–4).

> **Our greatest need is not to accomplish something, but to abide with Someone.**

He is the One who safeguards our rest. Our time with him is a relationship we must safeguard and cultivate each day. So we come first and foremost not to be like him, but to be with him. Being with him always leads to change; by his grace, it always leads to being like him. But first, we must take him at his word and simply "Come."

And if that isn't enough, he gives us this promise that he carries the yoke with us. Oxen in the ancient world were yoked together. One of the reasons Jesus' yoke is "easy" is because he is doing the heavy lifting, if we let him. It is easy because he is living in us and through us.

So today, before you do anything, don't forget to abide with Someone! Get alone with Jesus. Take time to pray. Read. Meditate on Scripture. Ask him to help you carry all that is heavy. And don't forget that you are not walking or working alone! Safeguard your rest by getting alone with the One who is our rest.

Today, let's look at ways you can safeguard your rest.

The Root of Our Rest

- How is the image of being yoked with Jesus helpful to you?

- What is the difference between getting away and getting alone?

- What is most wearisome to you that you need to ask Jesus to help carry?

- In what area of life do you need to resist the temptation of feeling that you need to accomplish something?

Let's examine Psalm 62:1–2. Read this portion of Scripture and then prayerfully reflect on the following questions:

- The psalmist calls God his rock and fortress. As you think about God's unchanging character, which of his attributes do you need to be reminded of most today?

- The psalmist equates rest with a Person, not just getting away to a different or quiet place. Why is this important to remember?

- In what ways is God's character meant to be rest for your soul?

- What is one practical way you can safeguard your rest this week?

Take a few moments to compose a prayer to God. Take your pain, your worries, and your weariness to Jesus. Remember that he is gentle and humble. He is a "Man of sorrows" (Isaiah 53:3 NKJV). He knows what it is like to be tired. Ask him to help you carry what feels impossibly heavy.

• My Prayer •

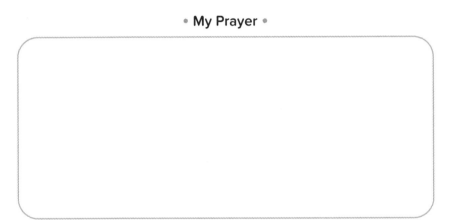

• Dig Deeper •

Listen to *The Proverbs 31 Ministries Podcast*, "How to Overcome When You Feel Overwhelmed" with Rebekah Lyons.

• Highlighted Verses •

Truly my soul finds rest in God; my salvation comes from him. Truly he is my rock and my salvation; he is my fortress, I will never be shaken.

Psalm 62:1–2

day 28

How to Overcome Procrastination

RUTH

For several years, while serving at a church in Ohio, we lived in a beautiful old brick home. It was located on a street with lots of trees. And our yard was no exception! The trees were beautiful to look at, but as we quickly found out that fall, they were also a lot of work to clean up after. Just when you thought you had all the leaves raked, more magically appeared.

So every fall, my husband would rally the troops to begin the long process of cleaning up the yard. This usually took days. Sometimes weeks. And our troops? They were our four young children. As you might imagine, they weren't exactly enthusiastic or overly energetic about the mission.

In an effort to educate and inspire them, my husband came up with the "Three Cs" of hard work. They weren't terribly sophisticated and not entirely exhaustive, but the Three Cs were enough to begin changing their perspective about work. Which was needed, because it would have been easy to keep pushing this mission back—until, hopefully, the wind blew the leaves into the neighbor's yard!

"Work hard until the job is COMPLETE," I'd hear my husband chanting. "Work hard without COMPLAINING," the battle cry would ring out. "And COOPERATE." There's probably more we could say or add, but that was enough for them at the time!

What they wanted was to either get the job over with or keep putting it off. What we might call procrastination. And it isn't too far off the mark to assume that most of us could use the Three Cs as adults.

Procrastination hits us all. No matter our age or the project or task, it is tempting to keep putting off whatever we have to do.

"Maybe this will take care of itself."
"I'll get to it tomorrow."

150

"I *really* don't want to do this."
And so on!

But procrastination not only robs us of the life we really want—a life we actually love—it also robs us of living out God's vision for work itself. In other words, procrastination is a deeper issue: how we see and understand work in general. We need to see it through God's eyes.

Overcoming procrastination changes when we *view* our work differently, not just *do* our work differently.

At the very beginning of the Bible, we read how God placed Adam and Eve in a garden. A garden with trees. He didn't place them there just for their enjoyment. He gave them work to do. In Genesis 2:15 we read that "The Lᴏʀᴅ God took the man and put him in the Garden of Eden to work it and take care of it."

What is worth pointing out is that this description of working in the garden happens before the fall—before sin entered the world. Why is that important? Because our work is good. It has meaning and purpose. After the fall our work becomes harder (Genesis 3:17–19), but it does not lose its significance. Or its sacredness.

> **Overcoming procrastination changes when we view our work differently, not just do our work differently.**

Work isn't just about us. While it is important to discover our unique gifts and calling, we also need to remember that, ultimately, our work is meant to glorify God and bless others. So no matter what we do, or have to do, it is meant to be an act of love and service to others.

Struggles with time management and the discipline to execute a to-do list point to a deeper problem. They are important symptoms to understand and address. But at the core of our struggle with work is our understanding of work. When we begin to view work as God does, we begin to see more clearly how we can overcome procrastination.

Today, let's take a closer look at whether we struggle with procrastination. Through the following questions and reflection prompts we'll discover simple ways to work hard in God's eyes.

Overcoming Procrastination

- Describe a time or season when you battled procrastination.

- What daily tasks do you notice are most difficult for you and why?

- Take some time to prayerfully consider what might be underneath your procrastination. Ask the Holy Spirit to reveal any idols that might be at the root of procrastination. For example, has comfort or pleasure become an idol?

- What is one thing you can begin doing this week to overcome procrastination?

A verse to consider when thinking of work is Genesis 2:15. Read and reread this verse as you reflect on the meaning of work in God's eyes. Once you have done this, reflect on the following questions:

Why is it significant that the command to work was given before the fall?

In what ways can our work become about us?

In your own words, describe the difference between how our culture views work and how God views work.

What is one practical way you can begin to see and pursue your work differently?

Take the next few moments to write out a prayer. Ask the Holy Spirit for help to overcome procrastination and to work to serve others. Pray for insight and a renewed desire to love God and love others as we should.

• My Prayer •

• Dig Deeper •

Read *Every Good Endeavor: Connecting Your Work to God's Work* by Timothy Keller.

• Highlighted Verse •

The Lord God took the man and put him in the Garden of Eden to work it and take care of it.

Genesis 2:15

day 29

The Best Decision-Making Advice We Can Give You

KAREN

Have you ever known someone who seemed to be so in tune with God that, as a result, they appeared to be so skilled at living? They made wise decisions, gave prudent advice, and their walk with the Lord was intimate. It was evident that prayer was intrinsic to their life, almost as vital as breathing. I first met someone like this when I was in high school, and it greatly fascinated me, making me want to study their actions to see what their secret was. This person was the pastor's wife at the little country church across the road from me.

Miss Pat moved into the church parsonage when I was in the ninth grade. I wasn't attending church anywhere, so she invited me to come to theirs. I soon began attending the church's youth group and playing on their softball team as the starting pitcher. This woman opened her arms to me, allowing me into her life to have a close-up view of how she behaved as a wife, mother, friend, and believer in Christ.

Well, she would be the first to admit that she wasn't a gourmet cook, a skilled interior decorator, or even a person who was book smart. Nevertheless, I saw an even more magnetic quality in her than any of those—she talked to Jesus as if he were her best friend and as if her very life depended upon knowing what he would have her do in each decision she made.

One thing I noticed early in our relationship was that this woman prayed about everything. She prayed for the people at church who were facing financial hardship or a major medical diagnosis. She prayed for the single woman who was contemplating whether the current relationship she was in was spiritually healthy for her. She prayed for daily provisions, and for her kids' teachers. Why, she even prayed when she lost one of her contacts in the bathroom sink! No matter or situation was too small for her to pray about.

Her brown leather Bible often lay open on her kitchen table as if she had just finished reading it. It was dog-eared, highlighted, circled, and marked up long before Bible journaling became a popular pastime of Christians. She was the poster child for the famous saying often attributed to Charles Spurgeon: "A Bible that's falling apart usually belongs to someone who isn't."[1]

One day I flat out asked her what the secret to living a successful Christian life was. Her answer was simple. "You realize that your very life depends on staying connected to Jesus above anything—or anyone—else. Don't make a move without him and always keep him as your first love." That was decades ago. She is now well into her seventies and still a mentor to me. And I have realized over the years how very true her advice is. If we want to be people who make wise decisions when faced with so many options, we need to tether our decision-making to Scripture and align our hearts with God every single day and with each individual decision.

> **If we want to be people who make wise decisions, we need to tether our decision-making to Scripture and align our hearts with God every single day and with each individual decision.**

Psalm 86:11 in the Amplified version of the Bible depicts such a person, a person who petitions God, saying, "Teach me Your way, O LORD, I will walk *and* live in Your truth; Direct my heart to fear Your name [with awe-inspired reverence and submissive wonder]."

In life, we must earnestly want the Lord's way, not our own. This begins with fearing him—what we learned on the very first day of this journey is the alphabet of life. I noticed a few other things about this descriptive verse.

It depicts the person who wants to know the way of the Lord declaring that they will *walk* and *live* in God's truth. These two words in English are just one word in the original Hebrew. This word helps clarify the verse for us. The term is *halak* (pronounced *haw-lak'*), and it has many shades of meaning. It doesn't just mean putting one foot in front of the other to propel yourself forward. It suggests you are accompanying, continually following, accessing, patrolling, and traveling.

This multifaceted definition really makes the word *walk* a vibrant verb! Look back over that list. When we walk in God's truth, we are accompanying him. But we aren't just walking by his side. We are continually following him. We have access to him as we walk, so we are not trekking alone. Nor are we sauntering obliviously. We are on patrol, watching out for what might be lurking around the next corner. We also are not rambling aimlessly. We are traveling through life with a final destination in mind, and we allow God to lead us there.

Let's pray for that with the awe-inspired reverence and submissive wonder described in the latter half of the verse. If we have humble hearts that truly want to seek after the Lord, we will take each decision, no matter how small or great, and ask the Lord to teach us to walk and live in his truth. As my mentor once told me, it is straightforwardly simple, but it also requires a spiritual strength to not trust in yourself—or just follow the suggestion of a friend or the advice of some expert in culture. God alone holds the answers to all of life's dilemmas. Let's purposefully and sincerely bring each decision to him before we pick up our foot to walk.

- In the journaling section below, work through a decision you are facing. It may be something at work, a situation with a relationship, a matter in your home, or a conflict with a loved one. First, list it below.

- Before doing anything else, spend some time in prayer. Use the words of Psalm 86:11 as a springboard. Here is an example:

Creator God, please teach me the direction in which I should go. My desire in this situation is not to get my own way. Rather, I want to walk and live securely in your truth. Please direct my heart and help me to sense your will in this situation. I revere you and I am in awe of you, and I want to submit to your wishes in this situation.

• **My Prayer** •

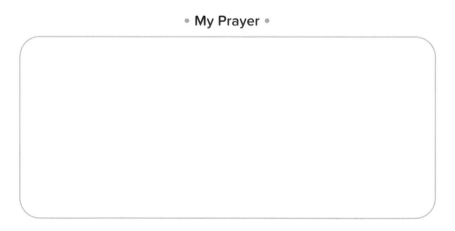

- Prayerfully think through your options. List them below without making a judgment on them. Merely state the various ways you could respond to this situation.

- While keeping a posture of prayer in your heart, read back over the list you generated. Ask God to reveal to you in the coming days which option you should choose. You don't need to decide this minute. You are only asking God to direct you to the best choice. Then, read through the following verses, and jot down other thoughts that come to your mind about making this decision.

  Proverbs 3:5–6

  Proverbs 18:15

  Psalm 25:4

  Colossians 2:6–7

Philippians 4:6–7

James 1:4–6

Now, go forth, following closely behind the Lord in anticipation of his answering your cry for help in this decision.

• Dig Deeper •

Listen to the *Rootlike Faith* podcast with Patrick and Ruth Schwenk, Season 1, episode 10: *"The Importance of Prayer (and how to pray)."*

• Highlighted Verse •

Teach me Your way, O Lord, I will walk and live in Your truth; Direct my heart to fear Your name [with awe-inspired reverence and submissive wonder].

Psalm 86:11 AMP

day 30

How to Dream Again

RUTH

Chasing dreams is hard when it feels like all you are doing is changing diapers. It's hard to think about your future when you are fighting unexpected health problems. And dreaming about how things could be different can seem impossible when you are in the middle of a painful divorce.

We can stop dreaming for different reasons. And certainly, in different seasons. Sometimes it's the big and ugly and devastating stuff. Other times, it is the relentless onslaught of day after day that wears down even the desire to think with hope about our future. Just getting through the day is enough!

Yet, our God is the God of the future. A God of new beginnings and new creations. A God who asks us to depend on him. To trust him and surrender to him. But he is also a God who works where he is welcome. He goes with us and promises to work through us.

Our dreams aren't necessarily *our* dreams; our dreams are God's desires lived out uniquely through us. So it is okay to dream, but we must always dream in the direction of God's will.

When we read the Bible, we are reminded, and should be encouraged, that the Lord is a God of hope. One of my favorite examples of this is found in the Old Testament book of Jeremiah. Jeremiah was a prophet, so he wasn't exactly the most popular guy! His job was to call God's people back to faithfulness. God's judgment was real, and of course, he loved them no matter what. But if they didn't return to the Lord, they would encounter his judgment, in the context of his good, but not always gentle, love.

In the sixth century BC, God's people were eventually carried into exile—they were taken from the Promised Land into seventy years of captivity in Babylon. But it is in the middle of those circumstances that God speaks hope. Promises a future. He is going to bring them back again. Their return to the land is coming.

Through Jeremiah, the Lord speaks to them and reminds them that even in exile there is an opportunity for a new beginning. In Jeremiah 29:11 we read, "'For I know the plans I have for you,' declares the Lord, 'plans to prosper you and not to harm you, plans to give you hope and a future.'"

Hard days can be filled with hope when we remember the heart of God.

While God's people are in exile because of their disobedience, one of the applications we can make is that he is not done with his people. He promises a future. We have a future not because of our faithfulness, but because of God's faithfulness. We can dream again. We can learn to love our life again because God is good and gracious. Hard days can be filled with hope when we remember the heart of God. And again, his heart is not only to be with you, but work through you.

It's okay to dream about what God wants for you. There is nothing wrong with wanting to be used by God. Our dreams will change depending on the season we are in. And dreams take time. They don't happen overnight. They require faith, but also perseverance.

So one of the questions we can ask ourselves today is, "What is God calling me to do in this season?" Or put another way, "What desire has God placed on my heart that he is asking me to say yes to?"

It's okay to dream—to dream in the direction of what God wants, not just what we want. Take some time today to prayerfully consider the desires and dreams you may have—or dreams you may have forgotten about.

Learning to Dream Again

- In what ways have you forgotten to dream and why?

- Do you ever feel guilty for dreaming? Why?

- How have your dreams changed with life's changing seasons?

- Why is dreaming in the direction of God's will so important? What does it look like, practically, to do that?

Let's consider a popular and oft-quoted verse, Jeremiah 29:11. But let's also keep it in its context. It is a promise to give Israel a future while in exile. It is an important verse because it reminds us that no matter what our circumstances are, God is faithful to us. And he is a God of hope who always promises us a future. He desires our faithfulness. As we seek the Lord, he is faithful to give us a future—a promise to be with us and work through us. Take some time to read Jeremiah 29:4–14. Then reflect on the following questions:

- Jeremiah 29:5–6 is all about settling into the town or city they are in. God was saying to his people, "You are going to be right here for a while. So plant a garden. Dig in and grow some roots." Why is this theme of being faithful right where we are so important when talking about future dreams?
- In verse 11, we see God's promise of a new future. Some of those living in exile would not see that promise fulfilled entirely or at all. Sometimes we see the fulfillment of dreams, and other times we don't see them completely. Why is this an important perspective to have?
- Why do you struggle with dreaming again?
- Prayerfully consider your future, with hope. What do you believe is one dream the Lord is giving you and why?

Take a few moments to write out a prayer. Ask God for a pure and sincere heart as you learn to dream again.

• My Prayer •

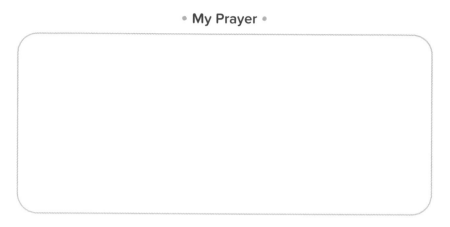

• Dig Deeper •

Listen to *The Alli Worthington Show* podcast, "How to Dream Again with Bianca Olthoff."

• Highlighted Verse •

"For I know the plans I have for you," declares the LORD, "plans to prosper you and not to harm you, plans to give you hope and a future."

Jeremiah 29:11

Finding My Follow-Through

It is of no benefit to come up with a strategy for living life well if you fail to find your follow-through. You have to implement what you've learned. In our final ten days together we will explore practical tips, life hacks, and even technological tools for getting life done without coming undone. Whether it is an evening routine that will help you have a better tomorrow, the strategy of smart sequencing, or methods for saving time and energy by working smarter, not harder, this final stretch will empower you to cultivate habits that position you best to carry out your responsibilities without neglecting your relationships. Most important, it will also present you with several ways to deepen your faith and develop a closer walk with Jesus every day. Grab your Bible and a pen and begin. You are so close to the finish line!

day 31

Getting Life Done without Coming Undone

KAREN

I often have the thought, "If only I could stop life for a few days—then I'd finally get all caught up." *{sigh}* Of course, this rarely is an option. How about you? Do you ever wish you could just stop life with all its work, errand-running, kid-raising, hubby-tending, crazy-busy activity and get your home decluttered and organized for once? Maybe just for three or four days no one would need you to cook, wash, help, answer, or do ANYTHING! Then you could take the time to sort through your closets, dressers, cupboards, garage, and basement and get rid of what you no longer need or use, and straighten up what is left.

One afternoon, a commercial popped up on the TV screen for a popular pain reliever. The line spoken by the actor in the thirty-second spot somehow made sense—and motivated me in this arena of getting chores completed. She declared something along these lines: "It's funny how much you can actually get done when it all *has* to be done." It made me think about all the times I've found myself in a situation where things "had to be done." Perhaps I was throwing a birthday party for a dozen of my child's closest friends, and they were going to be over in just a few hours. No procrastinating. No overthinking. I had to kick it into high gear and get the party rolling. I feel the same way when packing to leave on a flight and I can't be late to the airport. I dive in and pack like a madwoman. Or when our home was for sale and we were about to have a showing. I cleaned it thoroughly and in record time. The urgency of such upcoming events propelled me forward, making me work efficiently and lightning fast.

Since not all tasks around the home must be done with the same urgency, they don't seem to be accomplished at the same rate. I've scrutinized what my biggest obstacle is to accomplishing chores and performing overdue maintenance in the various rooms of our home. I actually think it is twofold. Either there is no event (or no boss) commanding that I get to it. Or I wrongly surmise that I need to have a long stretch of time available to tend to the many areas of my home and the numerous chores that beckon me. (I don't work well on projects in little snippets. If a task takes about five hours to complete, I won't work on it for ten days in a row a half hour at a time, as some of my friends do. Nope. I wait until my family is all gone, and then I dive in and work frantically for five hours straight, wrap it up, and move on to the next task.)

If you need some encouragement to become more self-motivated, don't look for a boss to tell you what to do; look to your future sanity and remember the ant.

Proverbs 6:6–8 gives us a glimpse of an industrious creature that is self-motivated and gets its chores done year-round—the ant! It reads, "Go to the ant, you slacker! Observe its ways and become wise. Without leader, administrator, or ruler, it prepares its provisions in summer; it gathers its food during harvest" (CSB).

No event-driven laboring here. There isn't even a boss in sight, yet the ant gets its chores done. The Hebrew word translated here as "prepares" is *kun* (pronounced *koon*) and it means to establish and make ready; to be steadfast, stable, or secure; or to make firm. And remember, the ant does this all without any outside prompting! He has ample provisions year-round because he is consistently diligent. If you need some encouragement to become more self-motivated, don't look for a boss to tell you what to do; look to your future sanity and remember the ant.

You may also want to try this little strategy that works well for me. I came up with an idea a few years back to help me take incomplete projects around the house from "to-do" to "it's done!" No boss is making me do it. And, as I mentioned, I often don't get started if I don't think I have oodles of time to work. However, this plan speaks to that time factor and helps me become motivated to move.

I decided to list all the organizational and cleaning tasks that needed attention around my home on a piece of paper. Then, I went back and categorized them by estimating the amount of time each would take. Some projects would require three or four hours to complete. Others could be done in about an hour, and still others might take me only fifteen to twenty minutes. Using the list-making feature on my phone, I put these tasks in groups, assigning each time category its own color and ranking them in order from those that would take the least time to complete to those that would take the most.

Now, when I have a chunk of time in my day, I can simply ask myself, "How much time?" For example, today I have an hour block between the time I am done with this entry of our journey and the time I need to start preparing supper. Before I'd done my categorizing exercise, my mind tended to think of these individual tasks as one huge combined project—a mountain my mind just could not climb—so I didn't attempt to do any of them. But now I know that if I have an hour block, I also have a project that will fit in that time slot. Or I could pick three projects from the list of fifteen- to twenty-minute chores and get them all done. So in a few minutes, when I shut my laptop, I will pull out the list, pick a project, tackle the task (or tasks), and then delete it from the list. Voila!

Think through the questions below to come up with your own list of chores, categorized by the length of time it will take to complete them. Then transfer the list to your phone for convenience. You don't need a boss telling you what to do. You can be industrious and self-motivated, just like the ant!

First, just brain dump the various projects you can think of that need to be done around your home. Don't try to put them in any order, just write them down as they pop into your mind.

Then, using the following labeled list, transfer the tasks to the proper category below. Once you've written a task below, cross it off the master list you generated above. You can also log these into a note-taking or list-making feature on your phone.

- 10 minutes or less
- 15 to 30 minutes
- 1 hour
- 2 to 3 hours
- 4 to 5 hours
- An entire 6- to 8-hour day

Look over your schedule for the coming week and identify a pocket of time—whether twenty minutes or two hours. Then, circle the task from the list above with a corresponding estimated time of completion that you will tackle first. Place it on your calendar. You can do it!!

Finally, in the space below, write out a prayer to the Lord about being self-motivated to get projects done around the house in an ant-like way.

• My Prayer •

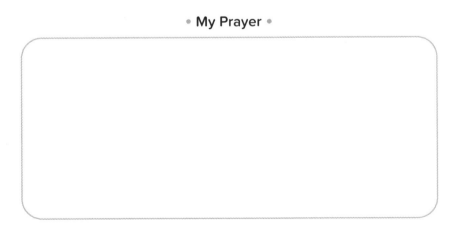

• Dig Deeper •

Listen to *The Lazy Genius Podcast* with Kendra Adachi, episode 322: "What to Do with Random Pockets of Time."

• Highlighted Verses •

Go to the ant, you slacker!
Observe its ways and become wise.
Without leader, administrator, or ruler,
it prepares its provisions in summer;
it gathers its food during harvest.

Proverbs 6:6–8 CSB

Three Things to Do Tonight for an Easier Tomorrow

KAREN

My daughter—once a four-year-old who loved to brush the hair of her dolls, her cousins, or any animal that would sit still—is now an award-winning stylist who owns her own salon. It wasn't just hair that she was fascinated with when she was younger. She also loved to dig in my purse, grab my lip gloss, and put it on while looking in the mirror. Today, as someone in the beauty industry, she helps women to unearth the most beautiful outside version of the inward soul that is uniquely them. And—as a bonus to me— she helps her mama in the fashion, hair, and skincare areas.

One time, as we were visiting out on her back deck sipping kombucha, she asked me what products I used on my face. A sheepish smile slowly crept over my face. You see, I don't use any products at all! My mom— who when she passed away at nearly ninety years old barely looked seventy—only ever used petroleum jelly on her face and nothing else. She used it to remove her makeup at night, and she put it on in the morning before putting on fresh makeup to greet the day. Since I couldn't stand that greasy stuff, I'd only used water and a washcloth to wash my face for all my decades of life.

Well, my daughter was not going to stand for that, and quicker than you can say "collagen cream with retinol," she was hooking me up with a three-step process centered on natural, clean products to use each night to ensure that my skin remained youthful and glowing and that any wrinkles were kept at bay. One is a cleanser, one is a pore minimizer, and the final one is a moisturizer. And so, to keep her happy—and hopefully look as young as my sweet mama did—I faithfully do all three steps each night before climbing into bed.

Psalm 90:17 talks about a different kind of beauty—the beauty of the Lord. "And let the beauty and delightfulness and favor of the Lord our God be upon us; confirm and establish the work of our hands—yes, the work of our hands, confirm and establish it" (AMPC). The beauty of the Lord isn't about an outward appearance. The original Hebrew word translated "beauty" is *noam* (pronounced *no'-am*) and means agreeableness, suitableness, delightfully pleasant, or absolute favor. The beauty of the Lord is also mentioned elsewhere in Scripture in Zechariah 9:17; Psalm 27:4; Isaiah 28:5, and elsewhere. But what I love about Psalm 90:17 is that the beauty of the Lord resting upon us is mentioned right along with God establishing and confirming the work of our hands.

> In Psalm 90:17, we find a wonderful pattern of prayer—asking the Lord in all his beauty, delightfulness, and favor to confirm and establish the work of our hands each day.

Just what is the work of our hands? The term in Hebrew for "work" here is *maaseh* (pronounced *mah-as-eh'*) and it has several layers of meaning. It can mean achievements, accomplishments, an occupation, or business acts, but it can also be used to refer to common tasks, practices, concerns, and deeds. For me, those last four words encompass much of what makes up the bulk of my ordinary days. I work with my hands, performing common tasks. I carry out practices that help my days run more smoothly. I may have a concern about a child who needs my attention, or just needs me to use my hands to hold them and reassure them everything will be alright. My hands perform deeds, especially good deeds done as to the Lord, the ones he has already planned out for me (Ephesians 2:10).

In Psalm 90:17, we find a wonderful pattern of prayer—asking the Lord in all his beauty, delightfulness, and favor to confirm and establish the work of our hands each day. And accompanying this prayer, I've implemented my own three-step regimen to carry out each evening just before bed that can help me have a beautiful day the next day. The three components of this process are the *button up*, the *head start*, and the *big three*.

As I begin my nightly wind-down ritual—which of course includes my three-step facial routine—I take time to go over the three actions that I can do tonight that will help me have a better tomorrow. First, I ask myself what I need to button up. Did I get interrupted while doing the dishes and wiping down the counters and not complete that task? It greatly frustrates me to wake up to a messy kitchen. I simply can't enjoy my morning cup of coconut mocha coffee while sitting at the dining table to read my Bible when there are dirty dishes ogling me from the sink. (This may not bother you. For you, it might be something entirely different.) Or perhaps I intended to deposit the four checks that have been sitting neglected in my purse, but never got around to it. I will think of one such task that I can take a few minutes to button up, checking it off my to-do list.

Second, I try to identify anything I can get a head start on that might only take me fifteen minutes or so. Could I brown the ground turkey for the sloppy joes I plan to put in the slow cooker first thing in the morning? Could I put all the kombucha bottles I need to return to the store in my vehicle and make out my grocery list now for more efficient errand running tomorrow? Simply getting a jump on one or two of the tasks I have planned can help the next day go so much more smoothly.

I finish up the three-step strategy by grabbing my planner and turning to the page for the next day. I ask myself, *What are my big three for tomorrow?* I know I might have over a dozen things I would like to accomplish. However, I try to simplify things and list only the top three tasks most imperative for me to complete. I may still have an ever-growing to-do list in the back of my planner. However, when I look at each individual day, I like to have my brain focus on only the three most crucial items. It helps me to feel my day is more doable when only three goals are on my mind. Of course, if the day turns out to be rather productive, I can always flip to the back of my planner for another task waiting to be done.

Try this three-step process yourself. Fill in the blanks below. Then, when you are doing your own nightly beauty routine, look at the list and complete the three-step process. It's guaranteed to help you experience a better tomorrow.

- **Button up:** One undone task of the day that I could complete before bed is _____.

- **Head start:** When I think about what I must accomplish tomorrow, I realize that I could get a jump start on a portion of the task by doing this tonight: _____.

- **The big three:** Although there are many items I could put on my to-do list for tomorrow, when I think of the top three actions most significant to complete, they would be _____, _____, and _____.

Now craft a prayer using Psalm 90:17 as a template. Ask God to help your work to be confirmed and established each day.

• My Prayer •

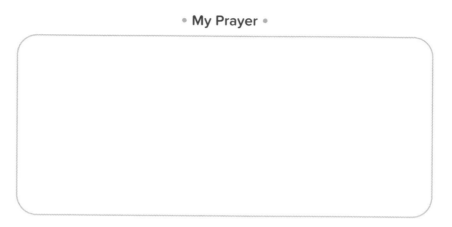

• Dig Deeper •

Listen to *The Candace Cameron Bure Podcast*, Season Four, episode 3: "Do Tough Stuff" with Bianca Olthoff.

• Highlighted Verse •

And let the beauty and delightfulness and favor of the Lord our God be upon us; confirm and establish the work of our hands—yes, the work of our hands, confirm and establish it.

Psalm 90:17 AMPC

day 33

Finding Your Unique
Plan of Attack

RUTH

My husband is a morning person. I am not. I find myself getting more creative as the day goes on, and I thrive at night! When we started writing books over ten years ago, this always bothered me. I had this image of every author getting up early, sipping coffee, and then writing their masterpiece!

So you can imagine my relief when I heard a well-respected and successful author share how he wrote most of his books after midnight. This was perhaps the first time I began to see and understand the importance of developing a unique plan of attack for my work—in this case, my writing. This is just one example of the importance of doing our work diligently, but also differently.

The Bible is full of encouragement to work hard (Colossians 3:23). We are warned not to give up or grow weary (Galatians 6:9). We are instructed not to be lazy (Proverbs 12:11). And we are reminded that our labor for the Lord is never in vain (1 Corinthians 15:58). There is wisdom and reward for those who work hard and smart.

What we do matters. And so does *how* we do it.

In Proverbs 12:11, we are told that "those who work their land will have abundant food, but those who chase fantasies have no sense." There is a reward for working hard. But as you know, working the land as a farmer requires working smart. There is a time to plant and a time to cultivate. There are different times and seasons when not only hard work is required, but different *kinds* of work are needed to have "abundant food." While we are called to work hard, we also need to work smart. We need a plan to push through and persevere that is unique to us—or maybe unique to the season of life we are in. What we do and how we do it might look

While we are all called to work diligently, our work might look different.

very different if we are single as opposed to married with a family. How and when we work might look different when we are young compared with as we age. And there are special challenges and adjustments that need to be made if we live with chronic illness. All these variables require a plan that is unique to us and to our circumstances.

While we are all called to work diligently, our work might look different. As you consider developing a plan of attack that is unique to you, here are a few questions to think about to help you not only work hard, but also work smart.

- When am I at my best?
- Am I a morning person or night person?
- Am I working from my strengths and gifts?
- Is my current work rooted in my calling?
- Is there "invisible time" that I can do my work that doesn't sacrifice time with family or friends? (Maybe this looks like thirty minutes here or ten minutes there, or maybe this looks like the hour before you go to bed and everyone else is asleep.)
- Are there health or physical limitations I need to accept and accommodate?
- Is this season a time for preparing or producing?
- Are there things in this season being sacrificed that shouldn't be? If so, how can I still be productive and realistic?

Today, let's focus on developing a plan of attack that is unique to YOU! As you consider the following prompts and questions, keep in mind that we are all called to work differently.

A Plan that Fits You

- What is unique about your season of life that is worth taking into consideration?

- Is there something you need to give yourself permission to stop doing?

- What are two or three unique circumstances in your season of life that you can use to your benefit?

- Write out below what an ideal week might look like that would help you live out your unique plan of attack.

A key passage for today is Proverbs 12:11. Read and reread this verse. Remember the contrast made between those who work hard and those who are lazy, or "those who chase fantasies." Consider how the example of the person working the land is helpful in thinking about working hard and working smart. Once you have done this, reflect on the following questions:

- What is the person who works the land being praised for in this passage?
- In what ways is this person working hard and in what ways is this person working smart?
- How are you most tempted to "chase fantasies" or wishful thinking in your work instead of working smart?
- Identify two or three practical ways you will begin to implement a plan of attack that is unique to you.

Take the next few moments to write out a prayer. Ask God to give you not only the wisdom to develop your unique plan of attack, but the grace to stick with it. Ask the Holy Spirit to help you be aware of what is most important in this season of your life.

• My Prayer •

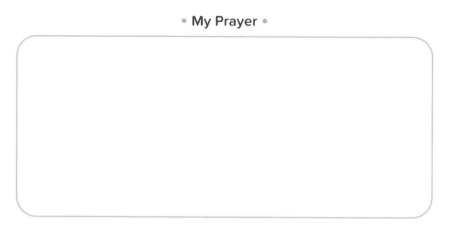

• Dig Deeper •

Listen to the *Rootlike Faith Podcast* with Patrick and Ruth Schwenk, Season 3, episode 15: "Learning to Be Faithful Where You Are."

• Highlighted Verse •

Those who work their land will have abundant food, but those who chase fantasies have no sense.

Proverbs 12:11

While we are called
to work hard, we also
need to **work smart.**

We need a plan that is
unique to us—or maybe
unique to the season
of life we are in.

What we do and how we do
it might look very **different**
if we are single as opposed
to married with a family.

How and when we work
might look **different** when
we are young compared
with as we age.

day 34

Smart Sequencing
and Habit Stacking 101

KAREN

I fell asleep in a heap of exhaustion that night, frustrated over the time it took me to get everything I needed done before bed. I just couldn't seem to get my act together. As a mom of three small children, a work-from-home woman, and busy wife, I was trying desperately to get it all done but felt downright defeated. What was I doing wrong? I lay in bed, pondering what I might have done differently to get more done in less time.

The tasks I needed to perform that night weren't anything out of the ordinary. However, they were many: make supper, do a couple loads of laundry, fill out permission slips for my kids' homeschool academy end-of-year field trips, wash the dishes, nurse the baby, return two phone calls, put the children in bed by myself since my husband worked nights, and send a birthday card to my grandfather. I worked furiously to get it all done, but a few tasks fell by the wayside and would have to wait until the next day.

Looking back later, I could see what my problem was: it was the order in which I did things. I first began by making supper, staying in the kitchen from start to finish. Then, when the food was ready, I fed the baby just before feeding my family. It was only then that I remembered the loads of dirty laundry calling my name. I put the first load in the washer. I filled out one permission slip and then put the kids in bed. Then I filled out the second one. Then I started to tackle the dishes, completely forgetting about the wash. The first load was done and ready to go in the dryer, but it didn't cross my mind until thirty minutes later. I tossed that load into the dryer and started the second load in the washer. Now I would have to stay up another forty-five minutes until the washer cycle had run its course and then the dryer did its thing on those clothes.

Overly tired from the activities of the day, I'd sat in the recliner and dozed off until I heard the ding of the washer. I'd then removed the first load from the dryer, transferred the second load to the dryer and folded the dry clothes before crawling in bed. I figured I would fold the remaining load in the morning, even though I really wanted to put all the clean clothes away before retiring. Oh, and I'd also need to fill out the birthday card and return the two phone calls the next day, since it had gotten too late to call anyone.

That evening was a perfect example of a situation we addressed yesterday—one where I needed to work smarter, not harder. I was working hard, all right. But I wasn't doing things in an order that made sense. I was playing whack-a-mole with the tasks, doing the one that popped into my mind rather than having a plan for intentionally doing them all in an order that helped to shorten the total time it took to get everything done.

> **We can take a cue from the depictions of order and time we see in Scripture and think through how to order our tasks so they are done in a manner that makes sense, frees up our time, and doesn't leave us exhausted.**

We get glimpses throughout the Bible of God being a God of order. He had a plan for the creation of the world, carrying out that plan in a particular order over the six days of creation (Genesis 1:1–31). Then, he rested from his work (Genesis 2:2–3). The early church was to do everything with decency and in order (1 Corinthians 14:40), and we are told that God is not a God of confusion, but of peace (1 Corinthians 14:33). In the book of Proverbs, advice is given about the order of tasks, telling us to do our outside work first before turning our attention to building our house (Proverbs 24:27). Ecclesiastes 3 is a chapter devoted to the concept that there is a time for everything. "There is a season (a time appointed) for everything and a time for every delight *and* event *or* purpose under heaven" Ecclesiastes 3:1 (AMP).

We can take a cue from the depictions of order and time we see in Scripture and think through how to order our tasks so they are done in a manner that makes sense, frees up our time, and doesn't leave us exhausted. I call this smart sequencing. So let's revisit my scenario above and see how things could have gone down so much differently by applying the concept of smart sequencing.

First, I could have started the first load of laundry as I began to prepare supper. At that time, I could have also brought the permission slips and the greeting card into the kitchen, filling them out at the table as I had a few minutes between food-prep tasks. During another break when making supper, I could have switched the first load of laundry into the dryer and placed the second load in the washer. Next, I could have nursed the baby, then fed my family. When dinner was over, I could have removed the first load of laundry from the dryer and folded it and placed the second load in the dryer. Then, while doing the dishes, I could've used a headset to make my phone calls. After putting the children in bed, I would've only needed to fold the last load of laundry and address the birthday card, maybe while watching a television show I enjoyed. I would have shaved at least an hour off my time by doing the tasks in an order that made the most sense.

Do you have any recurring chores around the home that might be more efficiently done if you applied the concept of smart sequencing? Let's explore that for a moment.

- What are some regular chores and responsibilities you must perform each night? List them all below.

- Looking at that list, write down the order in which you usually perform them or at least the order you remember last performing them in.

- Do you think that order makes sense? Might there be a different manner in which you could tackle them next time that would be an example of smart sequencing? Write the new order in the space below.

God cares about even the smallest aspects of our life. In the space provided, compose a prayer, asking God to help you be mindful and intentional about the order in which you perform your tasks around the house.

• My Prayer •

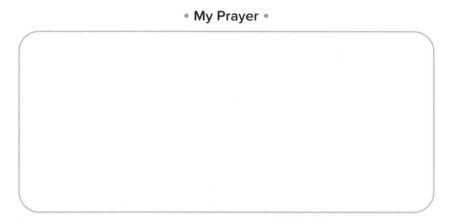

• Dig Deeper •

Listen to the *Life.Church Messages* podcast with Craig Groeschel, "Holy Habits: The Power to Change: Part 3."

• Highlighted Verse •

There is a season (a time appointed) for everything and a time for every delight and event or purpose under heaven.

Ecclesiastes 3:1 AMP

day 35

Three Simple Ways
to Achieve Long-Term Goals

RUTH

Any goals we set must be motivated by a heart that desires to love God and love others. When we set out on a new year or new season and begin to chart a course for our future, it should be done in humility before God. We are to "commit to the Lord" whatever we do. And what does God promise? That "he will establish your plans" (Proverbs 16:3).

Or as Proverbs 3:5–6 says, we need to "Trust in the Lord with all your heart and lean not on your own understanding; in all your ways submit to him, and he will make your paths straight."

So the first step in chasing any goal is to be sure it aligns with God's purposes. We ask ourselves the tough and honest question, "Is what I want what you want, Lord?" We labor in prayer, "God, purify me of any selfish ambition or desires." That is our starting point—a posture of trust and willingness to prayerfully seek the Lord with any goals we set. And to not "lean" on our own understanding, but in all our ways "submit to him." Again, the promise is that God is faithful, and he will make our "paths straight."

But how do we chase certain goals, especially the big ones, on a practical level? Once we have established that we believe these goals are not just our dreams but really do come from God, what then? And how do you turn one of those big and overwhelming goals into something manageable?

Let me offer three simple ways to make long-term goals achievable:

1. Begin by working backward. What I mean is starting with the end and then working in reverse. For example, if you have a deadline for a project or a big event you are planning for, start with when that project is due or the date of the event.

Once you have that on your calendar, you begin to work backward on your calendar. You take the details or the to-dos and assign dates to them. You begin to break all that needs to be done, prepared, or planned for into smaller deadlines. Now you have taken a long-term goal and broken it into more manageable short-term goals.

> **The promise is that God is faithful, and he will make our "paths straight."**

2. Begin to work in "chunks." These chunks are the short-terms goals you have just established and placed on your calendar. For example, let's imagine it is the beginning of September and you have a project due on May 1st. Working backward, you create deadlines at the beginning of each month that will help you accomplish the overall goal set for May 1st.

   Instead of getting overwhelmed with the long-term goal due on May 1st, begin to execute your short-term goals. Using our example, stay focused on accomplishing what is due October 1st, then November 1st, and so on. These are the chunks, or short-term goals, that will eventually enable you to accomplish the long-term goal.

3. Don't forget to work ahead—or at least keep your eyes on what is coming. As you are executing your plan each month, stay aware of the long-term goal as well. Work ahead as you have the opportunity. And if you are able, build in some time between the completion of your short-term goals and the due date of your long-term goal. This allows you a little buffer to take a short break and then return to what you are working toward with fresh eyes. It allows space to make any necessary changes or to accomplish something that was not planned for or anticipated.

Don't be overwhelmed by those long-term goals in your life! They are far more manageable than you might think. It comes back to budgeting time well and staying disciplined. It will require being organized. But with the right planning and some perseverance, you can do it.

Today, let's take some time to prayerfully consider the goals you have set. These might be for the workplace, or for your home and family. Maybe one is a dream you have always wanted to pursue. Whatever it is, let's explore how these three ways of making long-term goals more achievable might help!

Goals or Good Ideas

- How do you know if a goal is from God or just a good idea? What criteria can you use as you prayerfully consider setting goals?

- Which of the three ways to achieve long-term goals was most helpful and why?

- Write down one goal you are currently pursuing and something you know you need to change in order to achieve that goal.

- How can your goal honor God and at the same time be used to serve others?

Consider the words we read in Proverbs 16:3. Slowly and prayerfully read this verse. In this section, focus on learning to discern what God is doing in your life, or ways he is calling you to move forward in faith and faithfulness. Once you have done this, reflect on the following questions:

- What does it mean to "commit" something to the Lord?
- What role do other people play in helping us discern God's leading, or even in setting goals? See Proverbs 19:20–21 and Proverbs 12:15.
- What promise is found in Proverbs 16:3 that is encouraging to you and why?
- What is one goal you believe God is asking you to prayerfully consider either giving up or going after?

Take the next few moments to write out a prayer. Ask the Lord to give you wisdom to know what is from him and what may be from you. Seek his counsel on moving forward with goals that align with his will.

• My Prayer •

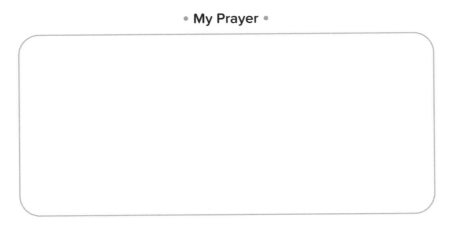

• Dig Deeper •

Watch the Saddleback Church YouTube video "Transformed: How to Set Personal Goals by Faith" with Pastor Rick Warren.

• Highlighted Verse •

Commit to the Lord whatever you do, and he will establish your plans.

Proverbs 16:3

day 36

How to Stop Being
Your Own Worst Critic

KAREN

I love to talk. Always have. Ever since uttering my very first sentence when I was eighteen months old—which my mom recalled being "Aunt Patty eats toast"—I have felt the need to comment on what was going on around me, give a running narrative of the thoughts in my mind, or entertain others with my storytelling antics. My teachers chided me for talking too much, especially when they were trying to teach a lesson. (In my defense, I thought what I had to share was way more interesting than what they were saying!) But my husband says my ability to talk—intentionally including others and making them feel comfortable—was what first attracted him to me. Of course, a few days into our honeymoon, he wondered if I was ever going to *stop* talking!

As with any personality trait, being someone who is verbose can be a strength that, when carried to an extreme, can become a weakness. We might use our words to encourage or teach. However, if left unchecked, it could lead to conversation dominance, barely letting others get a word in edgewise. But perhaps the greatest liability about my habit of forming words in my mind—and then letting them escape my lips—is that I can easily give a running monologue of criticism. Oh, not toward other people. My tendency toward pleasing people usually keeps me from blasting others. It's the critical thoughts I have on a loop in my mind, directed only at myself. I am my own worst critic.

There are many areas of life about which I beat myself up repeatedly. I'm discouraged by my eating and exercise habits. I scold myself for not always listening to others thoughtfully. I criticize myself for my inability to stop replaying past relational strains and failures in my mind. Why, I even berate myself for my inability to use up that bunch of celery in the fridge before it goes bad, thereby causing me to waste money! (Excuse me while I check Pinterest for "tasty recipes for celery" right now.)

Constantly criticizing myself leads to experiencing feelings of defeat. It sidetracks my day and cripples my productivity. It can also keep me from experiencing true rest, because I can't shut the thoughts off. Thankfully, my earliest mentor in the Christian faith taught me an important skill that helps to halt the negative thinking and dwell instead on the power of God available to me as a believer. That skill is Scripture memorization.

Memorizing Scripture helps snap my brain to attention, bringing it in line with God's thoughts about me. This is so crucial when my own thoughts have run amok—when they have started to accuse and bully, keeping me from feeling loved by God and tempting me to feel like an absolute failure.

> **Committing God's Word to memory is powerful. It helps halt the pattern of ungodly and negative thinking and ushers in the truth we so desperately need to hear, believe, and live.**

Scripture memorization is worth the effort. If you have never felt you could be successful at memorizing a verse or two, just think back to the oldies songs you might love. I'll bet you can sing them all from memory. Well, if we can memorize songs, we can memorize Scripture.

This past year one particular verse has been at the top of my mind. Whenever I feel the inner critic starting to chatter away, I recite 2 Timothy 1:7 in the Amplified version of the Bible: "For God did not give us a spirit of timidity *or* cowardice *or* fear, but [He has given us a spirit] of power and of love and of sound judgment *and* personal discipline [abilities that result in a calm, well-balanced mind and self-control]."

Doesn't this translation of this verse give you hope? Which one of us couldn't use a spirit of self-control, and who doesn't want a calm, well-balanced mind?

An interesting bit of Bible trivia is that the original Greek word for the phrase "sound judgment and personal discipline" is a single word that is found only in this verse and nowhere else in Scripture. That word is *sóphronismos* (pronounced *so-fron-is-mos'*). The Amplified version of this verse, written above, does a wonderful job of delineating what this single word means. In addition to having sound judgment and personal discipline, it also means to exercise wise discretion, or to be proper, prudent, and wise minded.

And so, when that scolding voice in my head tells me I have no power to resist temptation, I can recite this verse out loud to remind myself that God has already given me a spirit of self-control. When my thoughts begin a dance of worry, and I fear that I might make a wrong decision, I can again confidently recite this verse, reassuring my worried heart that God enables me to have sound judgment. When my heart starts to fret over the actions of another—which are out of my control—hearing my own voice declaring that God has already given me a calm mind helps me to settle down and obtain one.

Spend some time this week searching for verses you will commit to memory that you can let bubble up to the surface whenever your own inner critic comes calling. Committing God's Word to memory is powerful. It helps halt the pattern of ungodly and negative thinking and ushers in the truth we so desperately need to hear, believe, and live.

Look up the following verses. See if one of them resonates with you as one that would be beneficial for you to memorize. Circle the reference of the one you choose. Then, in your own handwriting in the space below, copy the verse. Decide to commit it to memory. A few suggestions have been given below to help you do just that.

- Philippians 4:8
- 2 Corinthians 10:5
- Colossians 3:1-4
- Proverbs 4:23–24
- Romans 8:5–6
- Ephesians 4:20–24

Now, write the verse you chose below:

Tips for memorization:

- **Put it on repeat.** Using the voice memo app on your phone, or another such voice recording platform, read any verses you want to memorize out loud multiple times in a row, making sure to also give the reference such as, "Philippians 4:8." Then, when you are doing the dishes, folding laundry, or out for a walk, listen to the voice recording and say the Scriptures out loud with it. The repetition helps to solidify the words in your brain.
- **Make it stick.** Use sticky notes to give you visual reminders to practice your verses. Place them on your bathroom mirror, the dashboard of your vehicle, or on your computer screen. But don't write out the entire verse. Write the verse but leave out key

words, replacing them with a blank. For each sticky note, choose different words to turn into blanks. Seeing these throughout your day will help you to recall and then store the words of the verse in your soul.

- **Keep a progress journal.** Purchase a pretty journal, and once you have memorized a verse or passage, write it down in your journal, along with the reference. It is encouraging to see the verses stack up.

Turn your thoughts into a prayer, asking God to enable you to hide Scripture in your heart so you can combat any thinking that weighs you down.

• My Prayer •

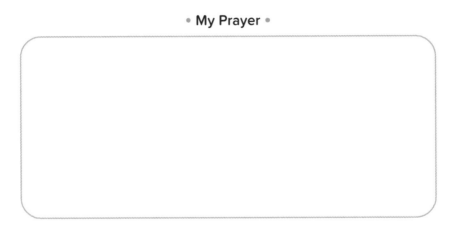

• Dig Deeper •

Listen to *The Scripture Memory Podcast*, episode 3: "Top Ten Memory Tips and Techniques."

• Highlighted Verse •

For God did not give us a spirit of timidity or cowardice or fear, but [He has given us a spirit] of power and of love and of sound judgment and personal discipline [abilities that result in a calm, well-balanced mind and self-control].

2 Timothy 1:7 AMP

day 37

Tips, Tools, and Technology to Grow Your Relationship with Jesus

KAREN

I was sitting with my family in church with my Bible and journal open, studiously taking notes on the morning's sermon. However, out of the corner of my eye I saw something that made my mama blood begin to boil. My teenage son was looking down at his cell phone in his hand, a big no-no during church! I shot him "the look." (You know what that is if you are a mom—or can remember your own mom's countenance when she was displeased.) It was then that my inattentive son rolled his eyes at me, which further made my blood boil. That is, until he slowly lifted his cell phone and pointed the screen in my direction, showing me what was on it. It was a Bible app that he'd used to look up the passage the preacher was teaching on! He was paying attention after all.

I had to smile. My nearing-middle-age self at that time had never thought about looking at a Bible verse on a phone. My, how times have changed! About a year after that, I myself began to use a Bible app to read and study my Bible. Not all the time. I still love the feel of my physical Bible in my hands with its smooth goatskin cover. However, I have come to believe that technology indeed can help us in our quest to grow spiritually. The trick is keeping it in perspective and not allowing the device to distract us, sending us to other places to gather trivial bits of information or causing our brains to temporarily turn to mush.

The spiritual growth of a Christian is a long-haul marathon and not a sprint. With each passing day, we have the opportunity to deepen our walk with Jesus as we pursue both more knowledge of God's way and a life lived in godliness that reflects our Savior.

How descriptive 2 Peter 1:3 reads in the Amplified version of the Bible: "For His divine power has bestowed on us [absolutely] everything necessary for [a dynamic spiritual] life and godliness, through true and personal knowledge of Him who called us by His own glory and excellence." God not only calls us as Christians to live a life of godliness that glorifies him, he has provided everything we need to do it! The phrase in this verse that is translated to "everything necessary" is the Hebrew word *pas*—which surprisingly is pronounced just like it is spelled. It means each, every, and all. This broad term means *all* in the sense of each and every part that applies to the whole. The total picture comes into view when we think of it in this way: amassing one individual piece at a time to form a whole.

As I look back over my own spiritual life—which now spans nearly four decades—I see how this long-haul journey has in many ways amassed one individual piece of the spiritual puzzle at a time. I first learned the importance of reading the Bible when I initially placed my trust in Christ at the age of sixteen. I remember getting off the school bus, walking through the neighbors' backyard to my own property and then running up the hill. I flung open the garage access door and dashed into my bedroom to flop down on my bed and read from the Bible the little country church had given me when I met Jesus.

> **All the relationships, biblical messages, studies of Scripture, and lessons learned through technology can combine to help us grow in godliness as we utilize the tools that can deepen our affection for the Father, Son, and Holy Spirit.**

After a year or so, I wasn't just reading the Bible, I was studying it by attending the Wednesday night adult Bible study at that same church, even though I was still a teen. Soon I began to memorize verses. Then came college, where I grew fascinated by the process of discovering the meanings of words from the original languages the Bible was penned in—Hebrew and Greek. I also learned about connecting with other Christians to support and serve, and reaching out to those who did not yet know Christ to display the gospel through my words and by my actions. Along the way, God has used many people, messages, methods, and now even technology to help me learn to grow in godliness. All the relationships, biblical messages, studies of Scripture, and lessons learned through technology can combine to help us grow in godliness as we utilize the tools that can deepen our affection for the Father, Son, and Holy Spirit.

Let me share with you some of my practices and resources that have helped me to grow in the areas mentioned above that might also be of benefit to you.

- **Learn to rely daily on the Holy Spirit.** Followers of Christ have the Holy Spirit dwelling within them (1 Corinthians 3:16). The Holy Spirit is our Helper. He teaches us and helps us to remember the things we've learned about Christ (John 14:26). The Spirit brings conviction (John 16:7–8). And he is a seal upon us as believers, a sort of down payment on the eternal life that is to come (Ephesians 1:13). When we are at a loss for how or what to pray, the Spirit intercedes for us (Romans 8:26–27). More than any other resource to help you grow spiritually, the Holy Spirit is the most crucial and effective.

- **Get connected in a local and biblically sound church.** Don't live in a Christian bubble, never interacting with people who do not follow Christ. However, it is imperative that you have a close inner circle that includes believers who are serious in their pursuit of Christ. So, if you haven't already, get connected with a church. Join a Bible study. Join a ministry and serve. Seek out others who will help to grow your faith because they also want to grow in theirs.

- **Speaking of friends, enlist the help of one as you seek to memorize Scripture.** One of my close friends also has a desire to memorize Scripture. So we leave voice messages for each other on a walkie-talkie app called Voxer, reading our Scriptures out loud each week. The accountability is so helpful, and doing it with someone else makes it fun.

- **Set yourself up for spiritual success.** Just as someone who struggles with overindulging in alcohol stays out of bars—and away from parties where there is a focus on drinking—set yourself up for spiritual success by cutting yourself off from places, people, or online locations that might trip you up in your particular struggle. If you are tempted to spend too much time on social media, delete the apps from your phone so you will need to access an actual computer and enter your login and password to go on the site. Sometimes having to jump through a few hoops helps us to see it's not worth it. If there are any unhealthy relationships you have, begin now to distance yourself from those people, asking God to bring along friends who will help, and not hinder, your spiritual growth.

Now, put pen to paper and construct a prayer to God, asking him to help you continually put all the pieces together that will propel your spiritual maturity, helping you to grow in godliness.

• My Prayer •

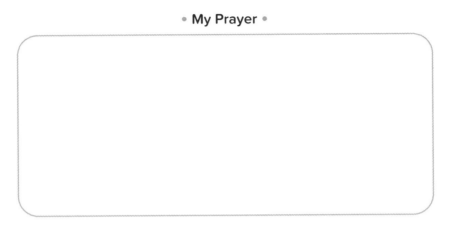

• Dig Deeper •

Helpful apps:

- For Bible reading: *BibleGateway* by HarperCollins Christian Publishing, Inc.
- For Bible study: *First 5* by Proverbs 31 Ministry
- For Prayer: *Echo Prayer* by The Parable Group and *PrayerMate— Christian Prayer*
- For sermons, podcasts, and reading plans: *iDisciple* by iDisciple LLC

• Highlighted Verse •

For His divine power has bestowed on us [absolutely] everything necessary for [a dynamic spiritual] life and godliness, through true and personal knowledge of Him who called us by His own glory and excellence.

2 Peter 1:3 AMP

day 38

The Three Best Habits for Getting Things Done

RUTH

Getting things done doesn't happen by accident. We need to work hard. And smart. But getting things done also requires the right habits.

An easy way of thinking about a habit is that it is simply a pattern of behavior. For example, you might be in the habit of reading every night before bed. Or maybe you brush your teeth every morning when you wake up. In Christians, the Holy Spirit uses habits or disciplines to build godly character and virtue in our lives. A habit might be a family eating together every night at the same time. Habits are important in so many different ways in our lives.

We also need habits if we are going to get things done, whether at home, in our personal lives, or in the workplace. So what are some of those habits that are helpful? Let me mention three.

First of all, we need to be in the habit of guarding our purpose.

This requires that we have clarity on our calling; we must be living out of this calling and chasing the right goals—committed to tasks or responsibilities that align with our purpose. It means we are intentional about not allowing external things to always dictate our time and energy. Guarding our purposes means we are careful not to allow others, especially those with strong personalities, to derail us from what is most important. One simple way to guard your purpose is to get in the habit of reviewing your purpose or your goals each week.

Second, we need to be in the habit of asking for help.

Don't be afraid to delegate. When we are not living out of our calling, we tend to spend more time and energy focusing on compensating for our weaknesses. But being in the habit of asking for help means we gather others, build a team, or delegate. This habit allows us to stay focused on what is most important—and to work effectively and efficiently. Again, a simple way to build this habit in your life is to ask yourself each week, *Where do I need help*?

And third, we need to be in the habit of getting over upsetting others!

The truth is, when we are living on purpose and setting the appropriate boundaries, others will be upset sometimes. For example, when we say no to serving or being involved in a group or ministry, people might not understand or may wrongly interpret our answer. When we are unable to help or commit to a project that might be good or important, others may be offended, question our loyalty, or think we are not all in. So we need to be in the regular habit of remembering where our approval comes from and not be swayed when people are not pleased with us (Galatians 1:10).

> **It's not just what we do but who we do it for that matters most.**

As you seek to be a person who gets things done, don't forget who you are really serving. Don't lose sight of who we are ultimately called to honor. In Colossians 3:17, we are reminded that all our work, "whether in word or deed," should be done "in the name of the Lord Jesus." The apostle Paul writes, "And whatever you do, whether in word or deed, do it all in the name of the Lord Jesus, giving thanks to God the Father through him."

Today, let's take a closer look at each of the habits we discussed above. And let's be honest about habits we need to change in our life.

Habits that Help or Habits that Hurt?

- How would you describe the habits in your own life?

- What habits are hurting you most and how?

- What habits are helping you the most and why?

- Which of the three habits discussed above are most important for you to focus on right now and why?

A key passage for today is Colossians 3:17. Here, the apostle Paul is talking about our work. He is reminding us that no matter what we do, who we do it for is most important. Sometimes it is easy to lose sight of who we are serving when we are focused on getting things done. It's not just what we do but who we do it for that matters most. Prayerfully read and reread this verse, asking the Holy Spirit to speak to you. Once you have done this, reflect on the following questions:

- What does Paul mean by working at something "in the name of the Lord Jesus"?
- What does our work look like when we are "giving thanks"?
- How can wanting to get things done be dangerous in our spiritual life?
- What is one way you are feeling led to change how you see your work or the desire to get things done?

Take the next few moments to write out a prayer. Pray for a heart that desires to love God and love others, even while getting things done. Ask for wisdom on what habits are helping you and what habits are hurting you.

• My Prayer •

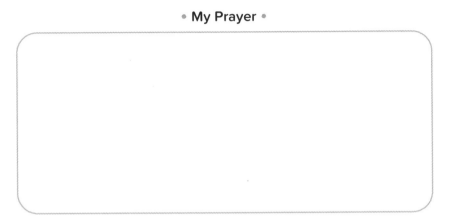

• Dig Deeper •

Read *Atomic Habits: An Easy & Proven Way to Build Good Habits & Break Bad Ones* by James Clear.

• Highlighted Verse •

And whatever you do, whether in word or deed, do it all in the name of the Lord Jesus, giving thanks to God the Father through him.

Colossians 3:17

day 39

How to Hit Restart
When You Get Off Track

RUTH

I'll be the first one to admit when I have gotten off track. My intentions can be good. Priorities are on point. I know exactly what I need to do and what I need to say no to. And then a day happens. Or a week. I find myself falling short and failing miserably at what I said I was going to do. So much for the life I love!

Here is where we need to be patient with ourselves. Not such a harsh critic. We might say we need to be compassionate with ourselves. We all need to be okay with hitting the restart button. We're all pursuing this life we love, imperfectly. Failures are going to be inevitable. And that is okay. It's what we do with those failures that matters most.

The real question is not whether we will fail, it is whether we will get back up again.

Failure is a universal experience. In many ways, we experience failure far more often than we experience success—which is what makes failure so dangerous and discouraging. It holds the power to break our hearts and steal our hope, tempting us to just give up! Failure has a way of exposing the gap between who we are and who we wish we were. Failure is everywhere we look because failure is everyone's experience.

So what do we do when we fail? How do we start again and avoid the discouragement that can come when we miss the mark?

Proverbs 24:16 gives us a clue of how to restart: "For though the righteous fall seven times, they rise again." Sounds simple? Yes—and no!

What makes getting off track so hard and discouraging is that we are tempted to just give up, throw in the towel or feel like we have to start from scratch. But this wisdom in Proverbs is simple because of this principle of getting up or beginning again that enables us to keep going.

We are going to fall or fail, the writer is telling us. And so, we need to "rise again." What else can you do that may be helpful to stay the course? Here are some very practical things to do the next time you need to restart:

- Begin again—but don't feel like you have to start from scratch. Just "rise again" where you fell or failed. Each moment or each day is an opportunity to experience God's mercy and grace.
- Evaluate why you go off track.
- Consider ways to protect your priorities to avoid future pitfalls.
- Ask God for his grace and wisdom to move forward according to his plans, not just yours.
- And finally, trust that God is still at work no matter what!

A good place to end this section is with the gospel and the reminder that we are loved, even in our failure. This theme of failure and restarting is at the heart of the good news of God's love for us. Jesus tells us in Matthew 5:3 that it is the "poor in spirit" who inherit the kingdom of God. It is those who know they have failed and need God's forgiveness who become citizens of God's kingdom and sons and daughters of God's family.

> **Our failure is always met with God's grace and mercy.**

So you are in good company! All of us have sinned and all of us have fallen short (Romans 3:23). Our failure is always met with God's grace and mercy. This is important to remember in every area of our life. Even when we are talking about priorities and living on purpose.

We are first and foremost children of God. Loved and accepted by him. All that we do, or want to do, is a response to his love for us. We hit restart not just for us, but because ultimately, we want to live a life that is worthy of the One who first loved us.

Today, let's take some time to discover where we are getting off track and how we can begin to hit restart.

Getting Back on Track

- Where are you getting off track with your priorities most often?

- As you prayerfully consider where you fall or fail, why are you most vulnerable in that area?

- Would you consider these failures to be related to schedule, something spiritual, or do they have physical causes (for example, insufficient sleep, health concerns, poor diet, not getting enough exercise, etc.)?

- What is one emotion you feel most often when you get off track and why?

A helpful Scripture on this concept is Proverbs 24:16. Take some time to read this verse. In particular, prayerfully read and reread the phrase "rise again." Once you have done this, reflect on the following questions:

- Where are you most tempted to give up and why?

- What does it look like practically to "rise again"?

- What is one way you can resist discouragement this week if you get off track?

- What are one or two ways to safeguard your priorities this week so you don't fall?

Take the next few moments to write out a prayer. Confess the ways you've fallen and failed. Ask God to give you the strength to begin again and depend on him completely.

• **My Prayer** •

• Dig Deeper •

Read *Overcoming Spiritual Discouragement: The Wisdom and Spiritual Power of Venerable Bruno Lanteri* by Fr. Timothy Gallagher.

• Highlighted Verse •

For though the righteous fall seven times, they rise again.

Proverbs 24:16

Five Ways to Carve Out Time for God, Every Day

KAREN

Bravo! You have made it all the way to the final day of our trek together to pursue our passions, cultivate habits of productivity, and refuel with times of rest. Let's end with the most important action we can perform each day: carving out time to be with the Lord.

One of the questions I am most frequently asked is "How do you connect with God during your day?" Although that is a question that simply can't be answered in a one-size-fits-all response—because we each are in different seasons and live different lives—I do have some encouragement to share with you by way of strategies and methods I have gathered over the years. Without a doubt, I can tell you what the first step is: BE PREPARED.

The well-worn saying is true, "If you fail to plan, you're planning to fail." This is especially true when it comes to carving out a few moments during your day to connect with Jesus. No plan? No time with him. That is often how it goes.

Years ago, when I first responded to the gospel and began my walk with Jesus, I discovered how imperative it was that I spend time with him reading and studying the Bible, praying for myself and others, and just being still in his presence all alone. Older Christians warned me not to be legalistic about it by insisting on a time of day or length of time for these meetings. I also learned that there wasn't only one method, book, or devotional I should read as part of this time. But I did come to understand how crucial it is to be prepared. We will have a much greater success rate if we plan ahead, putting our appointments with God on our calendar just like any other important meeting, and have all the resources and tools we might need in one place, ready to utilize when we have time in our day to meet with Jesus.

Hosea 10:12 speaks about our quest to seek the Lord during our days in terms of growth and gardening: "Sow righteousness for yourselves and reap faithful love; break up your unplowed ground. It is time to seek the LORD until he comes and sends righteousness on you like the rain" (CSB). For our last little word study in the original languages of the Bible, let's look at the Hebrew word in this verse that translates to our English word *seek*. It is *darash* (pronounced *daw-rash'*). This word doesn't just mean to look at something or someone. Its broad definition can mean one or all of the following: to care, to study, to inquire, to consult, to investigate, to ask or question, and to search carefully for.

> We will have a much greater success rate if we plan ahead, putting our appointments with God on our calendar, and have all the resources and tools we might need in one place, ready to utilize when we meet with Jesus.

Isn't this the goal of our time with Jesus? We show him our care and love as we praise him during our time spent alone with him. We study his words. We consult with him, inquiring what we should do about various situations. We investigate Scripture, carefully searching for his will, and asking him questions about following hard after him. And—much like a gardener—we need to be patient, allowing the seeds that have been sown to grow into a harvest of faithful love. Sometimes we need to break up the unplowed ground, exploring new territory with the Lord. Sometimes this territory is unfamiliar or even frightening. But he is there all along. As we seek him, he sends righteousness on us like the rain.

Here are five tips to help you develop a personal and consistent time with God:

1. **Release any pictures of perfection from your mind.** You know those images. They pop into your brain because of how you envision someone else's time with God looks, or what you've seen on social media: a well-worn and perfectly color-coded Bible open on a lovely porch. The sun is gently breaking through the clouds, illuminating the pages. A cup of steaming coffee is snuggled up next to the Scriptures. It looks like a scene straight out of a movie! Now, I'm not saying that I don't enjoy a cup of coffee on the porch when I read my Bible and pray. I may even post a picture of it. What I mean is that we have to get familiar with non-picture-perfect times of quiet with the Lord because they are much more common than the social-media-worthy ones.

   When my kids were small, I sometimes would go to the local fast-food restaurant so they could jump in the ball pit and split a large order of fries while I did my Bible study for the week. I've met with God on the sidelines of a baseball field while my son had a warm-up session for his travel baseball double-header. I've spent time praying in a coffee shop between medical appointments. I even have a waterproof Bible that I sometimes read while I was soaking in the tub or sitting at the beach while watching my kids play. The goal is not perfection. The goal is consistency.

2. **Reexamine your schedule.** Another notion we have ingrained in our brains is that time alone with God must be at "O-dark-o'clock" before anyone else is awake. But everyone has a different schedule. Think through your commitments for the coming day each night before you retire. Identify what block of time might be best for you to read, study, or even memorize Scripture and spend time praising God and praying. It may be early in the morning, last thing before bed, or sometime in between.

3. **Break it up into smaller portions.** Our connecting with God does not need to be done all in one fell swoop. Break it up into smaller portions. I like to do it by utilizing prayer prompts. I might pray for a certain relative each time I brush my teeth. When I drive into the city to do my shopping, I pray for another loved one. When I drive back home to my small town, yet another person—a struggling friend—is the subject matter of my petitions. I leave a few Bibles out around the house, ready to be perused when I have a few minutes. One is on the coffee table in the living room, another on my desk in my office, and a third on my nightstand. I might work on Scripture memory as I am in the waiting room at the dentist. We might not be able to spend an entire thirty to sixty minutes with God in one stretch, but if we break it up, we may still be able to meet that time goal by the day's end.

4. **Assemble a TAG basket.** TAG stands for Time Alone with God. I began to keep everything I would need for these one-on-one meetings with my Creator—my Bible, a notebook or journal, pens, etc.—in one place as soon as I became a believer. In college, they went into my backpack so I could take them to the library or out to a bench in a quiet corner of campus. Once I got married, I switched to a canvas tote bag. For years after that, I used a vintage basket I found at a yard sale. Then it was an old repurposed wooden card catalog drawer from a local library that I found at an antique store. All of these I could grab and take to a quiet space in my house or out on my porch or deck to spend time with Jesus. Today, I also tuck in note cards and stamps in case God brings someone to mind and I want to send them a handwritten message of encouragement. So gather your own items and make a TAG basket.

5. Use your ears. Another way to make sure you have a steady in-take of Scripture is to broaden your thinking about Scripture from reading and studying it only to also include hearing it. At first, I used to listen to the Bible on a set of CDs. Now there are many ways to listen to Scripture. It can be online, through an app, or with an audiobook subscription. When you have times of waiting, such as in the carpool line, or at those times when you are doing something truly brainless like folding laundry or weeding the gar-den, you can use your ears to take God's Word into your soul.

Now make it a matter of prayer. Ask God to help you creatively carve out time each day to grow your relationship with him.

• My Prayer •

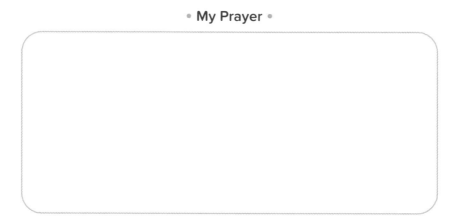

• Dig Deeper •

Listen to the *Lessons from the Farm* podcast with Nicki Koziarz, episode 72: "The Un-Quiet Quiet Time."

• Highlighted Verse •

Sow righteousness for yourselves
and reap faithful love;
break up your unplowed ground.
It is time to seek the Lᴏʀᴅ
until he comes and sends righteousness
on you like the rain.

Hosea 10:12 ᴄsʙ

A FINAL WORD

We have come to the end of our forty-day excursion. We hope you have found the time you spent reading, studying, and reflecting to be helpful in your quest to live your priorities and love your life. Now it's time for one final exercise. Please don't skip this part! It is the last piece of the puzzle, designed to help you keep your commitment daily to be deliberate in implementing what you have learned.

For this final assignment, you will need a pen, this book, some stationery or a note card, an envelope, and a stamp. Find a place where you can be alone for about thirty minutes. Begin by leafing through the book from start to finish, reminding yourself of the various topics of each of the forty days as well as some of the exercises that most stood out to you. (You can also review what you recorded on the Notes for Loving My Life pages.) Was there a particular prayer you wrote that speaks to your heart right now? Is there a reflection question whose answer was rather enlightening for you? Did one of the forty days stand out as a lesson you most need to recall and apply currently in your life? Try to determine the one or two most impactful aspects of this journey for you.

Then, take time to write your future self a letter. Recall the truths you learned or perspectives you gained through these forty days. Use your own words to encourage yourself to keep growing and keep going, implementing what it is you gleaned from the study. This will be a wonderful reminder to live out your priorities.

When you are finished, seal up the envelope and address it to yourself. Don't forget to include a stamp. Then, give it to a trusted friend. Ask them to mail it to you on a day somewhere between three months and one year from now. It can be on whatever day they feel prompted to send it to you. What a wonderful reminder it will be when you receive it to reevaluate and readjust if needed, and to keep deciding daily to live your priorities in a way that honors God and draws others to Jesus.

Thank you again so much for the honor of walking beside you in this forty-day journey. We pray it has been not only inspirational but also has equipped you in practical ways. It has been our joy to serve and support you. Mind if we pray for you?

Father, thank you so much for the friend now reading the words of this prayer. We praise you for her diligence in working through this forty-day challenge expectantly and with an open heart. Continue to propel her toward spiritual growth. Help her to crave your Word each day, taking in each morsel of truth she encounters. Increase her affection for you. Deepen her prayer time. Expand her sphere of influence. May she love and serve those in her life without neglecting the tasks you have called her to do each day. May she sense your presence, feel your approval, and experience your peace. We thank you for your hand on her life and for the ways you walk with her daily, teaching her to be more like your Son, Jesus. It's in his name we pray, amen.

In His Great Love,
Karen and Ruth

Notes for Loving My Life

Section One: Determining My Priorities

_____

_____

_____

_____

_____

_____

_____

_____

_____

_____

_____

_____

_____

_____

_____

_____

_____

Notes for Loving My Life

Section Two: Finding the Proper Perspective

Notes for Loving My Life

Section Three: Pursuing the Passions God Has for Me

_____

_____

_____

_____

_____

_____

_____

_____

_____

_____

_____

_____

_____

_____

_____

Notes for Loving My Life

Section Four: Finding My Follow-Through

_____

_____

_____

_____

_____

_____

_____

_____

_____

_____

_____

_____

_____

_____

_____

_____

LEADER'S GUIDE

A learning experience is greatly enhanced when you process the information alongside other people. The added insight and various perspectives of others not only stretch your mind, but also encourage your heart. If you desire to make this forty-day experience something a group of women does together, below is a simple guide for you to utilize as you serve as a facilitator. But first, here are a few suggestions as you gather your group:

- To locate other women who might want to partake in this forty-day experience, don't just think of friends, family, or fellow church members. Leverage your social media account to inform more people of the opportunity. Snap a picture of the book's cover—or a cute selfie of you holding the book—and post it, inviting others to join you. Provide a way for them to let you know they are interested in attending. You may do this by telling them to send you a direct message on social media or by sharing an email address. If you don't want to use your personal email address, you can create a new one to be used only for the study.

- In your promotional information, state that the study will be held over an eight-week period and that you will meet once a week.

- As you decide what day and time works best for your group, plan on ninety minutes of meeting time per week. This will allow plenty of time to work through the five days' content you will cover at each meeting and to toss out additional group discussion questions included on the following pages.

- Select a location that works well for the group. You might choose to meet in a home or church classroom, but if the group is small enough, you could also gather at a coffee shop or private room at your local library.

- Decide if you will provide childcare, or if you will leave it up to the individual members to arrange for this themselves.

- You may keep the meetings simple as far as refreshments go, encouraging each woman to bring along their favorite beverage to sip while you gather. Or take turns providing a simple snack along with a beverage. You, as the group's facilitator, provide this the first evening and then have volunteers for the remaining seven sessions. To make it easy, use an online site, such as Sign-up Genius, that will allow members to choose a date and will also send them an email reminder, so they don't forget to bring their refreshments.

- Optional: You may decide to form a Facebook group for the members of the study. This will be beneficial in a few ways. First, everyone can hop on there to introduce themselves before your first meeting. This way, you won't need to take time out of the meeting to do that the first week. It also would provide a central location for all information, updates, and schedule changes. If the group members allow notifications from the group, they can easily follow along with what is happening.

- Most important, begin now to pray for the members of your group, asking God to help you all learn how to prioritize your passions, cultivate productive habits, and refuel with times of rest.

Structure of the Weekly Meetings

Here is a suggested structure for the ninety-minute timespan for your weekly meetings. It is only a suggestion. Feel free to adjust, rearrange, add extra time, etc., based on your group's individual desires or needs.

> Intro and ice breaker: 10 minutes
>
> Sharing highlights of the five days of content: 60 minutes
>
> Weekly action step questions: 15 minutes
>
> Closing prayer: 5 minutes

If your group decides to do weekly refreshments, have these ready fifteen minutes before the start time. Encourage those who can come a little early to grab something to eat and drink and then visit with each other before the session begins.

Eight-Week Study Outline

Week One: Days 1–5

Intro and ice breaker: 10 minutes

(If your group does not have a Facebook group where members have already introduced themselves, this section may take a little bit longer on the first night.) Have each member introduce themselves, telling just a little bit about where they are in life as far as family, employment, responsibilities, and roles. Have them also answer this icebreaker question: What is your go-to order right now from a coffee house?

Sharing highlights of the five days of content: 60 minutes

This week covers the first half of section one, Determining My Priorities. Spend 10–12 minutes on each of the five days in this section (Days 1–5), asking members to share what most inspired, encouraged, or challenged them.

Weekly action step question: 15 minutes

Many of us have never thought about living our priorities intentionally. We tend to just take life as it comes, trying to tend to all our relationships and responsibilities without a particular plan. After experiencing the first five days of this study, name one change you would like to make this week going forward to help you be more intentional.

Closing prayer: 5 minutes

Have one volunteer from the group close in prayer. Then, make sure you relay any information about the next meeting that the members need to know.

Week Two: Days 6–10

Intro and ice breaker: 10 minutes

Welcome the members and ask them to each share how they would spend their time on a Saturday if they had it all to themselves and could do whatever they wanted.

Sharing highlights of the five days of content: 60 minutes

This week covers the second half of section one: Determining My Priorities. Spend 10 to 12 minutes on each of the five days in this section (Days 6–10), asking members to share what most inspired, encouraged, or challenged them.

Weekly action step question: 15 minutes

This week we explored spending time with God, spending too much time with our screens, and navigating the tension between our responsibilities and our relationships. Is there an adjustment you'd like to make in any of these areas? Share it with the group.

Closing prayer: 5 minutes

Ask for a volunteer to close the group in prayer. Then share any announcements pertinent to the next meeting.

Week Three: Days 11–15

Intro and ice breaker: 10 minutes

Greet the members and ask them to each share what their favorite childhood toy or game was and why.

Sharing highlights of the five days of content: 60 minutes

This week covers the first half of section two, Finding the Proper Perspective. Spend 10–12 minutes on each of the five days in this section (Days 11–15), asking members to share what most inspired, encouraged, or challenged them.

Weekly action step question: 15 minutes

After spending time this week thinking about obstacles that might be standing in your way, what is one change you would like to make in your life to help you become better at managing your priorities?

Closing prayer: 5 minutes

As you close, have one member of the group share a prayer out loud. Afterward, make sure to cover any details for the class that members will need to know going forward.

Week Four: Days 16–20

Intro and ice breaker: 10 minutes

Welcome the members and ask them to share the best book they have read in the last few years and why they loved it.

Sharing highlights of the five days of content: 60 minutes

This week covers the second half of section two, Finding the Proper Perspective. Spend 10–12 minutes on each of the five days in this section (Days 16–20), asking members to share what most inspired, encouraged, or challenged them.

Weekly action step question: 15 minutes

After looking this week at how Sundays can help us find an effective rhythm, and determining some frustrations in our current schedules, is there one suggestion you want to implement or adjustment you want to make in your weekly routine?

Closing prayer: 5 minutes

Ask for a volunteer to close the group in prayer. Also cover any house-keeping or scheduling items for the group members.

Week Five: Days 21–25

Intro and ice breaker: 10 minutes

Let everyone know how glad you are that they are there. Then, have members share what three toppings they would choose if they were ordering a pizza all by themselves and didn't have to consider what any friends or family members wanted.

Sharing highlights of the five days of content: 60 minutes

This week covers the first half of section three, Pursuing the Passions God Has for Me. Spend 10–12 minutes on each of the five days in this section (Days 21–25), asking members to share what most inspired, encouraged, or challenged them.

Weekly action step question: 15 minutes

The last five days covered not only determining your passions, but also goal setting and how to stop being paralyzed by perfectionism. Has this week's study given you any ideas for an action step you would like to implement in any of the areas covered? If so, share it with the group.

Closing prayer: 5 minutes

Close out your time together by having one member of the group share a prayer. Be sure to also share any information the group will need for the next week.

Week Six: Days 26–30

Intro and ice breaker: 10 minutes

After welcoming the members, go around the room and have each person tell the group their very favorite television show—past or present—and what they most love about it.

Sharing highlights of the five days of content: 60 minutes

This week covers the second half of section three, Pursuing the Passions God Has for Me. Spend 10–12 minutes on each of the five days in this section (Days 26–30), asking members to share what most inspired, encouraged, or challenged them.

Weekly action step question: 15 minutes

So many topics covered this week! From how to say no, to safeguarding your rest, to decision making and overcoming procrastination. Is there an area that jumped out at you where you most need to modify your behavior or mindset? Share your thoughts with the group.

Closing prayer: 5 minutes

Have one volunteer from the group close in prayer. Then, make sure you relay any information about the next meeting that members need to know.

Week Seven: Days 31–35

Intro and ice breaker: 10 minutes

Let's talk holidays! Ask the members of your group to share the holiday they most love celebrating and why. It can be from their childhood or from their current season.

Sharing highlights of the five days of content: 60 minutes

This week covers the first half of section four, Finding My Follow-Through. Spend 10–12 minutes on each of the five days in this section (Days 31–35), asking members to share what most inspired, encouraged, or challenged them.

Weekly action step question: 15 minutes

The final two weeks of this study are very practical in nature. Did you learn a practical tip, idea, or strategy from this week's five days of content that you want to implement?

Closing prayer: 5 minutes

As you close, have one member of the group share a prayer out loud. Make sure to cover any details for the group that members will need to know going forward.

Week Eight: Days 36–40

Intro and ice breaker: 10 minutes

Time to play "Would you rather?" Have members answer this question, explaining why they chose the answer they did: Would you rather get a pampering pedicure, have a hot-stone massage, or take an uninterrupted three-hour nap?

Sharing highlights of the five days of content: 60 minutes

This week covers the second half of section four, Finding My Follow-Through. Spend 10–12 minutes on each of the five days in this section (Days 36–40), asking members to share what most inspired, encouraged, or challenged them.

Weekly action step question: 15 minutes

Of the practical topics covered in the last five days of the study, is there a tip, tool, or strategy you are excited about implementing in the future? Share your answer with the group.

Finally, ask the members what they thought about the exercise at the end of the book that instructed them to write a letter to their future selves. Take a poll of how many did it. Ask them their thoughts about how this exercise may help them to maintain momentum in the future.

Closing prayer: 5 minutes

Ask for a volunteer to close the group in prayer. Then share any announcements pertinent to your group, such as if you will keep in touch on a group page or have a final get-together just to socialize.

ENDNOTES

Introduction

1. Dr. Henry Cloud, *The Law of Happiness: How Spiritual Wisdom and Modern Science Can Change Your Life* (New York, NY: Howard Books, 2011), XII.

Day 3: Your Most Important Priority

1. St. Therese of Lisieux, quoted in Jacques Philippe, *Called to Life* (New York: Scepter Publishers, Inc., 2008), 15.

Day 8: Be the Boss of Your Screens

1. Harsha Kiran, *techjury*, January 3, 2024, https://techjury.net/blog/smartphone-addiction-statistics/.

Day 10: How to Stick to the Priorities You Set

1. *Fulton J. Sheen's Guide to Contentment* (New York: Simon and Schuster, 1967), 74.

Day 11: This Is What's Standing in the Way of Your Progress

1. Wendy Boring-Bray, reviewer, "What Is Rumination," *Mind Diagnostics*, October 30, 2020, https://www.mind-diagnostics.org/blog/repetitive-thoughts-and-behaviors/what-is-rumination.

2. *The Moody Bible Commentary*, ed. Michael Rydelnik and Michael Vanlaningham (Chicago, IL: Moody Publishers, 2014), 1010.

Day 12: The Danger of Sacrificing the Things That Matter Most

1. Stephen R. Covey, *The 7 Habits of Highly Effective People* (New York: Free Press, 1989, 2004), 98.

Day 14: Why Multitasking Is Killing Your Progress

1. Carey Lohrenz, "The Shocking Truth about Multitasking in The Age of Distraction," *Forbes*, June 15, 2021, https://www.forbes.com/sites/forbesbooksauthors/2021/06/15/multitasking-in-the-age-of-distraction/?sh=153b5c054918.

2. Carey Lohrenz, *Forbes*.

Day 15: You Can't Be Friends with Everyone

1. Henri J. M. Nouwen, *The Inner Voice of Love: A Journey Through Anguish to Freedom* (New York: Doubleday, 1996), 84.

Day 17: The Second Sunday Secret for a Productive and Peaceful Week

1. Brad Brenner, PhD, "The Mental Health Benefits of Having a Daily Routine," *Therapy Group of NYC*, September 30, 2020, https://nyctherapy.com/therapists-nyc-blog/the-mental-health-benefits-of-having-a-daily-routine/.

Day 20: One Simple Trick to Reset Your Brain and Regain Your Joy

1. Amy Sullivan, as quoted in "An Ode to Silence: Why You Need It in Your Life," *Cleveland Clinic*, August 6, 2020, https://health.clevelandclinic.org/why-you-need-more-silence-in-your-life/.
2. "Ode to Silence," *Cleveland Clinic*.

Day 21: Chasing Your What

1. St. Therese of Lisieux, *The Story of a Soul: The Autobiography of The Little Flower* (Charlotte, North Carolina: Saint Benedictine Press, 2010), 163.

Day 26: How to Say No, Once and For All

1. Tony A. Gaskins Jr., @TonyGaskins, Twitter, January 13, 2015, https://twitter.com/tonygaskins/status/555099171775328260.
2. "5297. Hupopheró," *Strong's Concordance*, Biblehub.com, https://biblehub.com/greek/5297.htm.

Day 29: The Best Decision-Making Advice We Can Give You

1. Leigh Ann Thomas, "45 Charles Spurgeon Quotes to Uplift Your Faith Today," Christianity.com, July 22, 2021, https://www.christianity.com/wiki/people/charles-spurgeon-quotes-to-uplift-your-faith-today.html.

KAREN EHMAN is a *New York Times* bestselling author of twenty-one books and a speaker who has been featured on TODAY Parenting, Redbook.com, Crosswalk.com, and YouVersion.com. She is married to her college sweetheart, Todd, and is the mother of six children: three biological and three by marriage—although she forgets which ones are which. Her most treasured title is that of Grandma Kit to her grandson, Jasper. She loves collecting vintage Pyrex kitchenware and feeding the souls who gather around her mid-century dining table, enjoying her county fair blue ribbon-winning cooking.

Connect with Karen:
KarenEhman.com

 @OfficialKarenEhman

@karenehman

@karenehmanofficial

RUTH SCHWENK is the founder of the popular blog TheBetterMom.com and the trusted author of several books, including *Jesus, Calm My Heart*, *Settle My Soul*, *Pressing Pause*, *The Better Mom Devotional*, and *Trusting God in All the Things*. Ruth is a Michigan football superfan and a self-proclaimed foodie. But her greatest joy is her family. She lives with her children, two adorable pugs, and their loyal Labrador retriever in the beautiful college town of Ann Arbor, Michigan.

Connect with Ruth:
TheBetterMom.com

@RuthSchwenkOfficial

@ruthschwenk

@thebettermom